See How They Sell!

See How They Sell!

Success in Real Estate Sales

Tamara Lee Dorris

Writers Club Press

San Jose New York Lincoln Shanghai

See How They Sell!
Success in Real Estate Sales

All Rights Reserved © 2001 by Tamara Lee Dorris

Writers Club Press
an imprint of iUniverse, Inc.

For information address:
iUniverse, Inc.
5220 S. 16th St., Suite 200
Lincoln, NE 68512
www.iuniverse.com

The individuals named in this book voluntarily participated in either a survey or formal interview that informed them that their name and information was subject to publication. Pre-publication notification was sent to all survey/interview participants, with options to revoke or revise their presence in the work. The views in this book are those of the author and interview respondents and not the views of the CALIFORNIA ASSOCIATION OF REALTORS® or any local, state, or national association of REALTORS® mentioned or unnamed.

ISBN: 0-595-19038-3

Printed in the United States of America

This book is dedicated to the professional growth and development of the real estate industry. It is in special recognition of the people who work hard, both behind the scenes and in the trenches, to make this industry what it is today; may you always excel.

CONTENTS

FOREWORD

Sir Isaac Newton said, "If I have seen further, it is by standing on the shoulders of giants." Real Estate's heritage is one of standing on the shoulders of giants: the men and women who toiled tirelessly to build the great organizations across the country and the world. They brought consumers the Code of Ethics, community zoning laws, a secondary mortgage market, the MLS, orderly markets, RPAC and they hired professional managers to run their organizations. These real estate professionals of the past were giants.

The challenge of today is that everywhere you look, things are in motion, creating new connections and new ways of seeing the world of real estate. To face this new world, the real estate practitioner must think in new ways as did the giants of the past. Today they must bring professional technological competence to their organizations and to the consumers. Organizations must be transformed to represent the cultural diversity of this country and the world. Consider that during the last half of the '90s, almost 40 percent of the increase in homeownership was due to minorities and immigrants buying homes. Professionals must help find and make the most of opportunities to work with people of varied ethnicity.

Like the real estate professional of the past, today's professional must continue into the future by making a positive difference in lives of people.

By Richard Mendenhall
2001 President
National Association of REALTORS®

PREFACE

If you have ever considered a real estate career, you'll want to read this book. While there are dozens of books available on how to be a real estate superstar, this one is different.

Here, you will learn the real ropes of real estate. The hands on, behind the scenes approach of what you need to do to enter, get, and stay successful in the highly competitive business of real estate sales.

This book will help you know how to proceed. In these pages you will be guided through the numerous aspects of a professionally successful career in real estate sales. You will hear from established and top producing agents and brokers, in their own words, what it takes to excel in this industry. Even if you have been selling real estate for years, there is always room for improvement, and what better way to improve than by consulting with a group of your peers, nationwide?

Many of the chapters offer additional hands-on assistance by providing exercises, check lists, sample scripts, and record retention forms, all designed to ensure your step in the real estate arena is well fueled for success.

Furthermore, the communications section has been especially designed to overcome some of the most common client objections that even seasoned professionals are challenged with each day.

If you've ever considered a career in the lucrative and rewarding real estate industry, now is the time to explore it further.

Good reading and happy selling,

The author

ACKNOWLEDGEMENTS

In sincere appreciation to the many REALTOR® brokers and agents who have shared their valuable time and insight, through formal interview, web survey, and casual conversation, to make this book available for anyone who holds an interest in the real estate arena.

Also, a special thanks to the National Association of REALTORS®, the California Association of REALTORS®, and all other state and local associations who help keep this industry profitable, ethical, and visionary.

To Luanna Vaughn, who offered her exceptional editing services, between listing properties and writing offers.

Finally, to you, the reader, who might already have business cards printed and listing appointments scheduled, or are considering a new career in real estate, the time is now!

INTRODUCTION

If you're reading this book, chances are you're a licensed REALTOR®, or considering the possibility. Real estate is a unique business, unlike any you've ever known before. It can be an incredibly rewarding profession for those determined to succeed. Unfortunately though, for every successful agent or broker, there is probably a dozen who have failed. To summarize in a paragraph, or even in a book what causes an agent to fail, would be impossible. However, what can be focused upon, is what it takes them to prevail. This can be accomplished by looking to those who have consistently tasted and maintained success.

It is under such premise that this book has been compiled. By looking to established agents, top producers, and brokers for answers and advice, anyone entering the real estate sales arena will discover a map that leads them on their way to professional success. Even seasoned REALTORS® will find this information a valuable resource reference.

Many of the chapters end with a useable worksheet that will help you to keep track of work-related records. Moreover, these worksheets will set the pace for your success. Use them, and then keep this book as a permanent resource guide and record-keeper that you can easily access, anytime.

Thousands of REALTORS® have contributed to the information contained within these pages, even though some have given indirectly and informally. Hundreds of top-producers and real estate professionals have participated in formal surveys and interviews that comprise the basis of this book. Industry leadership has offered helpful direction.

If you're serious about pursuing a profession in real estate sales, you've picked the right publication!

See How They Sell!

Includes usable worksheets

GETTING STARTED

"Man's mind stretched to a new idea never goes back to its original
dimensions"
Oliver Wendell Holmes, Jr. (1841-1935)

Professional Profile

Ted Breden, GRI,CRS,ABR
Tedsworld@ync.net
Firm: Century 21 Capital Realty, Inc., Chicago, Illinois
Years in Business: 22

"When I began my real estate profession 22 years ago, I was taught how to be
a real estate salesperson. I helped people buy and sell homes- to help them
make their dreams come true."

Now that you've made the decision to embark upon the often exciting and
unpredictable field of real estate, the first step is obtaining your license. In
order to sell or list real property in the United States, it is necessary to hold
a valid state-issued real estate license. It is also important to understand
the educational requirements needed to acquire a real estate license as well
as being aware of the entity controlling licensing procedures. And, of
course, commitment is paramount.

A real estate license is your ticket to sell. In and of itself, it can take you
only so far. It is, however the first necessary step in starting what can ultimately be a very rewarding and lucrative career. Many industries require
licensing that is generally proceeded by training and standards specific to that

field. For example, physicians and attorneys are required to have accredited university degrees and other stringent requirements, pass grueling tests, such as the state BAR exam, before they are issued a license to practice in their respective fields. Fortunately, while real estate licensure works on a similar standard, a college degree is not necessary, nor is the required education as time-intensive and, the earning potential matches most other professions.

Professional Profile

Bonnie Guevin, CRS, GRI
Bguevin@grolen.com
Bonnie Guevin & Associates, Incorporated, Manchester, New Hampshire
Years in Business: 13

"I am a broker, owner and a top producing agent in this market area. I complete 45-60 transactions a year as a single agent with no assistants or agents working for me. The one thing I can tell someone who is serious about getting into this business is to take this business seriously. Buyers and sellers rely upon our professionalism and knowledge to help them through the largest transaction of their lifetime. Real estate is a commitment and a business you will want to excel at."

A license to sell real estate can only be issued subsequent to successfully taking the Real Estate Exam for your particular state. Before taking the exam however, you'll have to meet the prerequisite educational courses. So what are the basic educational requirements necessary to qualify for the state exam?

Evidence of successfully completing college-level courses in Real Estate Principals is the general pre-exam requirement. Most states also issue minimum and maximum time frames that the courses must be taken within. For example, in the state of California, the minimum time for the Real Estate Principles course is 2.5 weeks or 18 calendar days. This same course however, can be found in many junior and state colleges and consist of 63 hours of learning. As a result, there are multiple educational options for would-be licensees to expedite this part of the pre-licensing activity.

With the advent of technology there are now ample opportunities to take the pre-requisite course(s), including many on-line courses. A simple Internet search for "Real Estate Schools," along with your state, will probably result in multiple links. Still, there are traditional colleges as well as a menagerie of accelerated schools that specialize in real estate training. These schools tend to be more costly than traditional community and state colleges, however, the benefit is in the amount of time saved. As with any educational endeavor, always take great care ensuring that the facility you have selected is reputable and appropriately accredited. The quality of the course you take, as well as the effort you put forth, will greatly determine your success on the real estate exam.

Once you have acquired proof of successful completion of the Real Estate Principles course, you may apply to take the real estate salesperson's exam. Exam fees in different states vary, however, again using California as the example, the fee is $60.00. Upon passing the test, there is another $90.00 fee, along with a $32.00 fingerprint-processing fee. In Florida, you must pass the test with 75% accuracy. Many states also require two additional courses be taken within the first 18 months of licensure. Please check with your State Department of Real Estate to ensure you are well aware of the pre-requisites, testing, fees, and continuing educational requirements.

While it is not necessary to know every nut and bolt of the inner workings of the real estate industry, it is a good idea to at least understand the entities at work behind the scene and how the Department of Real Estate will play a vital role in your career.

The Governor of each state appoints a Real Estate Commissioner. This person, usually someone experienced in the real estate industry, oversees the licensing regulations of the entire state. It is the required bureaucratic branch that all licensees must answer to with respect to licensed activities. It is also the long arm of the law when it comes to pulling licenses and putting people out of business when they choose to not play by the rules. Most state Departments of Real Estate Offices have a web site where staff may be contacted and more aspects of each state can be studied. The important thing to remember is this: the DRE is the entity that grants licenses and the same entity that can take them away.

The DRE is responsible for suspending licenses or putting licensees on probation, as well. Maintaining a license in real estate sales requires honest, ethical practices and when a licensee's activities have been questioned, or complained about by a consumer or other entity, it is the DRE that will investigate the case. The DRE also oversees the continuing education requirements mandatory to keep licenses in good standing.

GETTING STARTED

Department of Real Estate Telephone:_____

State License Requirements:_____ _____

(hours/courses) _____ _____

_____ _____

Real Estate Schools:

_____

_____

_____

_____

_____

_____

_____

_____

_____

EDUCATION

"The only thing that interferes with my learning is my education."
Albert Einstein (1879-1955)

The DRE requires that you maintain a consistent level of awareness through education in order to keep your real estate license active. This helps to ensure that you are better able to serve your clients and is referred to as "continuing education." While continuing education is clearly the one facet of learning that must be taken seriously in order to keep your license in good standing, it is but one of the educational opportunities available to real estate professionals.

There are four categories of education to consider: continuing education (required hours), designation training, technology training, and real estate or sales related seminars and training. It is important to understand the various means of professional improvement that are available to you and to realize how greatly they can contribute to your success in real estate sales. It is equally important to recognize that continuing education hours will result in a better overall understanding, awareness, and skill in your chosen profession.

Continuing Education

Professional Profile

Pamm Mills,CRS,GRI
mailto:Pamm@MillsTeam.com
ERA Pat Hance & Company, Ft. Lauderdale, Florida
Years in Business: 20

"Take as many continuing education courses as possible. Keep yourself current in the industry. Listen to tapes, shadow seasoned agents, and never stop learning."

Not unlike other professions, the real estate industry requires that sales associates and brokers maintain a certain level of knowledge and awareness as it relates to the way they do business. To verify that these professionals stay informed about the industry, there is a universal requirement for earning continuing education hours. Continuing education hours are courses that have been approved by the Department of Real Estate in each state and are deemed vitally important in assuring real estate licensees maintain a high standard of professionalism.

While the Department of Real Estate is a state-run entity that can vary significantly from one state to another, the majority of states require continuing educational hours be met by its real estate license holders. Unfortunately, many licensees wait until the last minute, then, in a frantic rush, scurry to earn the hours they need to renew their license. In addition to the unnecessary stress this invites (not to mention potential fines for late renewals) licensees do themselves a great injustice because it is more difficult to retain information that is learned under pressure, hence, many key components that could contribute to their professional productivity are lost in the frenzy.

The important fact to remember is this: Continuing education should be considered as a valid and worthy educational avenue for real estate professionals who plan on staying ahead of the game. Many top producers agree.

Professional Profile

Vaughn, CRS, Naplesre@aol.com
The Dream Team
Years in Business: 20

"The best tip to offer new agents is continual and massive amounts of education. Take courses or classes every chance you get."

When asked what advice established agents could offer new comers, continuing education, by choice, was one of the most popular answers. Successful REALTORS® realize that in an ever-evolving industry, staying smart and informed includes on-going educational efforts. Doesn't it make sense then that responsible and effective real estate professionals will want to take as many of these courses as possible?

As noted earlier, educational requirements vary from state to state. A general guideline is that new licensees will need to take an additional two courses within a certain time frame. These courses might be, for example, accounting, business law, or something similar. Additional course work will serve to contribute to your continued success. Then, approximately every following four years, you will be required to complete the standard 45-hours of continuing educational hours.

There will usually be options as to how to take these courses. Correspondence study and live lecture have been the most common and many states are now recognizing the value of on-line training, which is an extremely convenient alternative.

After completion of the requisite courses and following the proper procedure, the real estate license will be renewed. Some of the basic continuing education courses fall under the heading of Consumer Protection, Agency, Ethics, Trust Fund Management, and Fair Housing. Local associations of REALTORS® are among the best resources for learning the various options and requirements that may exist in each state and we will discuss the importance of being involved in organized real estate in the next chapter.

Remember though, while continuing education is a requirement to keep real estate licenses in good standing with the state, it is also an excellent opportunity to learn to be a more effective agent or broker. Top producers from all over the country agree that taking more continuing education than is necessary helped contribute to their success. On-going continuing education is the smartest choice of all.

Professional Profile

Judith Nusser, Broker Associate
mailto:Nusser@Gcnet.com
Coldwell Banker- The Real Estate Shop, Kansas
Years in Business: 20

"Strive for additional education, get designations- continue to improve or you will do grave injustices to your buyers and sellers."

In the real estate industry, many REALTORS® have earned the initials of respected designations on their business cards. These designations represent a variety of things, but the one caveat is that they must be *earned* before they can be promoted. Real estate designations may be equated to earning mini-college degrees. These designations are very specific to the real estate industry, yet they require efforts that result in a more informed, professional licensee, ready and willing to provide their clients with exceptional service and skill. Let's take a look now at some of the most common designations. You can find this list on the NAR website, which is provided at the back of this book under "Web Resources." With growing areas of specialization and specific group affiliations, this list is by no means exhaustive and you can refer to the appendix for additional resources.

The Accredited Buyer Representative (ABR)

A buyer's agent represents the buyer in a real estate transaction for a fee; just as a seller's agent is hired to obtain the price and sale terms sought by the seller. The ABR is the only nationally recognized designation for buyer's agents. NAR's Real Estate Buyer's Agent Council, 430 N. Michigan Ave., Chicago, IL 60611 312/329-8656.

Accredited Land Consultant (ALC)

These REALTORS® specialize in the sale of subdivision developments, urban and investment lands, farms and ranches. The ALC takes approximately two years to earn through NAR's REALTORS® Land Institute, 430 N. Michigan Ave., Chicago, IL 60611 312/329-8444.

Certified International Property Specialist (CIPS)

REALTORS® who hold the CIPS designation have been involved in a number of international real estate transactions. The CPM is offered by the Institute of Real Estate Management, 430 N. Michigan Ave., Chicago, IL 60611 312/329-6060.

Certified Real Estate Brokerage Manager (CRB)

The CRB designation is recognized in the real estate profession as the symbol of management excellence and is awarded to brokerage owners and managers. The CRB designation is offered by the Real Estate Brokerage Manager's Council, 430 N. Michigan Ave., Chicago, IL 60611 800/621-8738.

Counselor of Real Estate (CRE)

Real estate professionals who hold the CRE designation provide objective real estate advice to investors, builders and financial institutions. The designation is awarded to all members of The Counselors of Real Estate and is very exclusive. Members include practitioners of prominent real estate, financial, legal and accounting firms, as well as government and academic leaders. The Counselors of Real Estate, an NAR affiliate that offers membership by invitation only, on either a self-initiated or sponsored basis. Members include practitioners of prominent real estate, financial, legal and accounting firms, as well as government and academic leaders. The Counselors of Real Estate is located at, 430 N. Michigan Ave., Chicago, IL 60611 312/329-8428.

Certified Residential Specialist (CRS)

Real estate professionals derive general real estate sales knowledge, as well as learning mortgage financing and computer applications. The CRS designates salespeople who hold the CRS designation to specialize in listing properties, selling, and investing.

Graduate, REALTOR® Institute (GRI)

The GRI designation is a mark of distinction that earns a REALTOR® the respect and confidence from their peers and the general public. The GRI designation is offered by the NAR, 430 North Michigan Ave. Chicago, IL 60611, through the organization's state associations of REALTORS®. 312/329-3282.

Leadership Training Graduate (LTG)
Referral and Relocation Certification (RRC) Program

The LTG designation recognizes professional and personal development and is offered by the NAR's Women's Council of REALTORS®. The RRC designation, also offered by **Women's Council of REALTORS®** recognizes a professional's ability to build a corporate relocation business and develop a referral network. The WCR is located at 430 N. Michigan Ave., Chicago, IL. 60611 800/245-8512.

Professional Profile

Pat Kressin

mailto:Pkressin@homesbyStarck.com

Starck and Company, Elgin, Illinois

Years in Business: 11

"My firm has 16 offices and 450 agents and one thing I can tell you for sure is that it may take a while to get established. But, joining a group like WCR is invaluable for gaining support and keeping current on industry issues."

Society of Industrial and Office REALTORS® (SIOR)

The SIOR designation recognizes a specialization in commercial real estate. To earn the designation, members must complete two educational courses, provide five years of documented, full-time work experience and meet a specific dollar-volume in sales and number of transactions annually, as set by the local SIOR® chapter. The SIOR is offered by the Society of Industrial and Office REALTORS, 700 11th St., N.W. Washington, D.C. 20005 888/891-SIOR.

Each of these designations, as well as others, are given in conjunction with your local, state and national association of REALTORS®, which we will discuss more fully momentarily. For now, simply recognize that, as a real estate professional, designations demonstrate to your clients your outstanding ability, skill, and awareness about issues that matter most. They also exhibit professionalism and perseverance and command respect in the real estate industry.

Professional Profile

Cathy J. Sorenson

mailto:Cwsorenson@aol.com

Sorenson Realty, Incorporated., Cape Coral, Florida

Years in Business: 20

"At least 10% of your earnings should be spent on further education. When you stop learning in the ever-changing real estate profession, you are headed for retirement, planned or not."

Technology Training

Because technology plays such a vital role in the real estate industry it deserves and receives a chapter of its own. However, because education involves technology, and visa versa, it would be an oversight not to make some mention of it here. In the chapter that has been devoted to technology, a closer look will be taken on various issues, such as how using the Internet and email can increase REALTOR'S® business opportunities. Here however, we will review "basic training" of technology that is essential for any real estate professional. Notice how many of the designations listed above include technology training.

MLS

Each association, county, or region has something called a Metro List Service. How it is designed and operates varies from one region to the next. Essentially though, this is a huge database that houses information on properties that are active, sold, or pending sale. When you write up a listing and submit it to your broker, it will be entered into the big MLS system, thereby allowing REALTORS® all over your county or region to pull up information about the property for potential buyers to consider viewing.

The properties are listed in MLS by specific criteria so that agents and brokers may "punch in" certain attributes that fit their buyer's requirements. For instance, consider having a buyer who wants to purchase a three-bedroom, two-bath house, with a fireplace and a built in swimming pool. With MLS, it is possible to search only for properties that meet those requirements. Clearly, the more criteria demanded, the more narrow the search results. In other words, if the same customer wanted the three-bedroom, two-bath property to be located on 2.5+ acres of property, plus located within a particular geographical area, the search results might be dramatically reduced. By restricting the search criteria so specifically, the results have also become limited, leaving fewer properties available to show your buyers.

A later chapter will focus more upon working with buyers and showing property, but for now it is important to understand that effective use of the MLS service in your area is vital for selling real estate.

General Technology

Anyone in the real estate industry who plans on becoming and staying successful, will need to use a computer. All across the nation (and the world for that matter), real estate professionals are learning the positive benefits associated with technology. For starters though, it is important to understand how to operate a computer, work with the operating system (WINDOWS or MAC, for example), send and receive email, create a database, search the web, design flyers, and operate a variety of real estate-related software. So, *how* exactly does one acquire this kind of training?

The good news is that technology training is becoming increasingly easier to obtain, and add to that the fact that most software programs are becoming increasingly easier to use, hence the term "user-friendly." Many local and state associations offer their members basic computer training. Check with your local real estate Association or Board first. In addition, there are numerous books available that offer instruction on a wide variety of programs, at all different levels of learning. There are also an abundant amount of on-line classes, community college courses, and private computer schools. Many basic computer skills are easy enough to learn by simply experimenting, asking a co-worker or friend, and using the "Help" button that is included with most software programs.

Basic computer skills generally include a word-processing software, a desk top publishing software for making flyers, a comparable marketing analysis (CMA) program to keep track of clients, and email and Internet training. Since these are the most basic programs used by real estate licensees, they are usually the easiest to obtain training on.

In summary, we have seen that there are a variety of educational opportunities for real estate professionals that expand from required courses to specialized designations and technology training. The important thing to remember is that any successful real estate professional will seize each and every opportunity they have to learn and be better prepared to face the challenges of an always-evolving industry. Even those continuing educational courses that are required for license renewal should be deemed a valuable and optional opportunity for professional growth.

Use the page that follows to document your educational efforts. Keeping centralized records of this sort will serve to remind you of important dates you might otherwise forget, such as when it's time to renew your license. It also helps you keep track of the designations you have earned, and when they were acquired.

REAL ESTATE EDUCATION RECORD

License Number:_____Date:_____

Continuing Education
Date   Course Name/Location   Credits Earned

_____
_____
_____
_____
_____
_____
_____
_____
_____

Designations
Name of Designation   Date Earned

_____
_____
_____
_____
_____
_____
_____
_____
_____

Notes:

_____

_____

_____

_____

_____

_____

_____

_____

_____

_____

ORGANIZED REAL ESTATE

Up until this point, you probably aren't very clear on the difference between the terms "REALTOR®" and "agent," and whether one even exists. Often the general public, as well as new licensees, assume that a licensed agent is automatically a REALTOR®. If this were true, it would certainly make for a more integrated industry, but unfortunately, that's simply not the case. For starters, understand that all REALTORS® are also agents (or brokers), but that all agents are not necessarily REALTORS® (but they should be!). Simply put, a REALTOR® is an agent who has recognized the value and joined the ranks of organized real estate, hence, they are still agents, but they have earned the right to use the trademarked term "REALTOR®" as well. Becoming a REALTOR® provides opportunity for community involvement and volunteer leadership while simultaneously holding members to the highest standard of professional real estate practices. All of this directly relates to the three-tier structure that is always functioning, albeit sometimes staged seemingly behind the scenes, to ensure the overall well being of the real estate industry.

Professional Profile

Judie McConville
JudieMc@ivnet.com
Prudential McConville Realty, Ottawa, Illinois
Years in Business: 25

"Involvement in your local, state, and national association is so important. Networking and sharing ideas at all three levels is vital to becoming a true professional."

The Difference: Organized Real Estate

Taking the required courses, paying the necessary fees, and passing the real estate exam qualifies you to sell real estate. However, unless you become involved with your local, state, and national associations, you will not be authorized to consider, call, or promote yourself as a REALTOR®. Furthermore, you will be hard-pressed to find a broker who will allow you to put your license under his. In order to elevate yourself to REALTOR® status, you need only make the effort to join the ranks of the other prestigious professionals at the three-levels we will discuss.

It is becoming increasingly clear to the general public, through consumer awareness and education, that there is indeed a difference between doing business with someone who is merely a licensee and someone who belongs to the elite REALTOR® crowd. From this point on, we will use the term "REALTOR®" as synonymous with "agent," with the understanding that all agents referred to or quoted herein are also REALTORS®.

Local Associations

Generally speaking, a local association represents a county or an area in a particular state. Think of your local association as your close-to-home resource that will assist you with a compendium of your professional needs. While there are currently somewhere around 1800 local associations across the country, to try and categorize them would be literally impossible. Some local associations are large and represent a thousand or more REALTORS®, while many others are smaller with less staff and service a few hundred REALTORS® or fewer. Regardless of size, smaller local associations generally perform most of the same functions as the larger associations, but it is all relative to what the membership in each area demands.

Just as size has no national consistency, neither does the specific services offered. There are, of course, standard services that your local association will provide. For instance, your local association will be the resource your broker will submit your listings to so that they can appear in your local MLS. They also provide lock boxes, training, seminars, and assistance with continuing education. More and more local associations are playing an active role in assisting their membership to become technology-proficient by offering computer training. And others, are extending marketing assistance.

In Rocklin, California, the Placer County Association of REALTORS® has an incredibly innovative program in place called the "Gold Club." This program, under the Association Executive Cindy Picos, provides a marketing and promotional benefit for members that can't be beat. Through promotional mailings, preparations, and database management, Gold Club members can always be sure their listings and sales are well promoted. To find out more about how this program was developed, contact the Placer County Association of REALTORS® at: http://www.placercountyassociationofrealtors.com/

Local associations also work hard to keep their REALTOR® members up to date. Most Local associations hold weekly MLS and special broker's meetings. These are great opportunities to "pitch" your listings to other professional REALTORS® who may know of buyers. It is also the local association where you will purchase your contracts, join your state and national associations, and often purchase other items busy REALTORS® need such as sign riders and software. More and more associations across the country either feature a real estate "store," or are offering their members some kind of on-line access to the many necessary and promotional tools that REALTORS® want to work with (see Appendix B "Tools of the Trade" for products and resources).

Local associations generally take a very active interest in the local community and local politics, with respect to the real estate industry. Community efforts can include facilitating local REALTORS® to become involved in housing projects, charities, or consumer awareness. From the local level, there is generally a legal advocate who listens to what the local agents and brokers have to say about certain legal and legislative issues so that those concerns can be communicated with state-level advocates, who in turn will lobby real estate laws in favor of REALTORS® for the state, and in some cases, the nation.

Local Volunteer Leadership

Each local association has hired staff. The number of staff varies tremendously, but you can always expect to find an Association Executive. This person reports to a Board of Directors consisting of volunteers active in local real estate. The Board of Directors from each local association comprises the Board of Directors for the entire state. Generally speaking, the larger the membership (the number of REALTORS®), the higher number of Directors required.

Many well-established agents and brokers become involved in local volunteer leadership and join the local Board of Directors in some capacity. The reasons vary, but primarily, most would acknowledge it as an act of "giving back" to the community that helped them become successful in the real estate industry.

In addition, being involved with your local association, even if you don't fill a board seat, is an excellent way to network with other like-minded REALTORS®, as well as contribute in some manner to the community in which you are trying to establish yourself. Local leadership can also be elevated to a higher level.

Each local association annually elects an Association President who represents all of the REALTORS® belonging to that local association. The presidency is an enormous responsibility and is performed voluntarily. Because active involvement in the industry is required for leadership, these volunteers are simultaneously maintaining their client base, selling and listing properties, or brokers who are managing offices, or both!

William Johnson, one such leader, shares with us his insights on volunteerism. He is an inspiration for any REALTOR®.

Interview with a Local President

William Johnson, GRI, CRS

William@WilliamEJohnson.com

RE/MAX Associates, San Diego, CA

Years in Business: 13

"I have been a volunteer with the association since I was first licensed and it has made a measurable difference in my ability to provide both a good living and a higher level of insight into the complex world of real estate.

I believed that if I learned more, it would ensure an edge with my perspective clients. This has been born out over and over again. I began the real learning process when I first volunteered and was then able to visualize the breadth and width of the industry.

It makes me wonder why, in this business, so many people are more focused on the short gain (getting new business) as opposed to creating a knowledge-based future where the certainty of clients requires less marketing and less competition. I believed then and I believe now that knowledge is power.

I take the view that my clients are clients for life and that no matter where they are; they count on my counseling for any all real estate issues.

This is not just selling and buying property but proper planning for their major asset holdings. With the many volunteer meetings that would seem to take me away from my clients, by sharing my involvement, my meetings become an integral part of my client relationships.

Volunteerism has been a win-win situation for me. I just observed that the people I had the most professional respect for, knew more and were there to help me learn. I simply reached out for the golden ring that is there for everyone's' grasp. I would encourage all of you in the industry to reach out and seize one of the most important and empowering opportunities in your career.

For those of you who have, or will, lead in our industry, my hat is off to you for your commitment and my congratulations for your vision and insight of this most complex industry."

William's sentiments concerning the importance of industry involvement represent an eloquent example of how sincerely volunteer leaders take their responsibility and what a vital growth factor it can be for any REALTOR® who is serious about growing his business.

Professional Profile

Teri Terrell
Terit@pcfl.net
Realty Executives, Palm Coast, Florida
Years in Business: 12

"Be involved in what you believe in. Even if you don't have lots of free time to sit on boards and committees, you can always find a way to contribute something, and taking responsibility in the community is the best means of self-promotion."

State Associations

While local associations may merge together with one another or have policies and procedures unique to individual regions, state associations represent and support all local associations consistently, within one particular state. State associations are generally very involved with policy and law as it relates to the real estate industry. Furthermore, this is the entity responsible for lobbying real estate issues to the state legislature.

Much like a local association, the state association is comprised of a board of directors too. This board of directors will include each director found at the local level, particularly the President. Clearly, when a state has a large number of members, large boards of directors will result.

State Associations will hold "Director's Meetings," a few times through out the year. This is where leadership from across the state will convene and periodically branch out by committee to discuss important industry issues.

In addition, most State Associations hold some kind of annual "Trade Show," "Exposition," or "Tech Fair." This is a grand event that encourages all REALTORS®, directors, and association staffers from the entire state to come together. This is an exceptional opportunity to discover the newest trends, hear informative seminars, and "see" the new products and service available to the industry. There will usually be vendors set up in booths, ready to entice REALTORS® with contests and give-aways, with hopes of building good business leads. These kinds of events, even at the local level, are an outstanding way of meeting service providers and comparing one against the other.

Don't miss the opportunity to participate in the various events your local and state associations might offer.

Gary Thomas, President

California Association of REALTORS, 95,000 members

Broker, RE/MAX Real Estate Services , Orange County,

Number of Agents: 320

Years in Business: 26

1. Why is membership at the state level so important?

For several reasons state membership is important. With the combination of agents into a state wide organization, this gives REALTORS® effective political clout in Sacramento [state Capitol] It also gives us a combined force for legal challenges, education, professional standards, purchasing power, research and demographics as well as trends in industry and technology.

2. How much experience should a REALTOR® have before pursuing a role in leadership?

I think that the experience level needed for pursuing a role in leadership varies by the individual and their background. Some would say a minimum of five years in the business. I would differ and say that depending on the individual's education level, prior work experience, desire and drive determine when they are ready, not the calendar of their real estate career.

3. Is there a certain time period a REALTOR® should wait before becoming involved with the local community?

A REALTOR® should become involved in the local community as soon as practicable. As soon as they have their feet on the ground in their new career, I would encourage their involvement to help them learn the community, help shape the community, and create an asset that will enhance their career.

4. What are the most dramatic changes you've seen over the several years in the real estate industry?

I go back to when the purchase contract was one page, and that page had very little pre-printed information. Certainly litigation, and the reaction by the legislature has changed the contracts, duties and responsibilities of the agent. I have also seen companies grow from small 10 to 20 person firms to hundreds and thousands of agents under a single ownership. The consolidation, the freeing of information through technology and the sophistication of the business have changed the face of the industry.

At the state level, volunteer leadership becomes even more challenging because you are coming from a local level, more accustomed to local issues. Consider an up-state New York local association president elected to state level and the different practices, policies, and procedures that would need to be learned. Clearly, real estate practice would vary between rural towns and New York City, for example.

Professional Profile

Wendy Furth
Wendysworld@juno.com
Coldwell Banker, Northridge, California
Years in Business: 16

"The most that you can ever hope to accomplish is "to make a difference". Being involved in the association at the local, state and national levels allows me to roll up my shirt sleeves and work on issues important to property ownership rights, assist in the development and stay on the cutting edge of technology and be ready to "make a difference" wherever and whenever I am needed."

The largest state association in the country is the California Association of REALTORS®, with over 95,000 REALTOR® members. The 2000 President, Richard Gaylord, a RE/MAX broker from Long Beach who has played a vital role in California real estate issues, acknowledges that he wasn't always involved in local or state politics. In the business since 1978, Richard finally recognized the value and the reward that came from community involvement and made an on-going commitment to the industry. When asked what the term, "REALTOR®" meant to him, his response was automatic:

"REALTORS® are held to a higher professional standard and subscribe to a higher code of ethics." His advice to new REALTORS®? "Absolutely get involved, it helps the industry, gives you professional exposure, and makes a difference!"

National Association

The National Association of REALTORS® (NAR) is where everything comes together. This is where the state leadership, both volunteer and paid, from all the states nationwide, unite. NAR is also the entity that plays a vital role in federal legislation. The NAR web site (see Appendix A) is also an excellent resource for REALTORS® located anywhere in the country.

The NAR web site contains a link to information about each states' Association, and you can find out important real estate related news headlines, read the NAR on line publication, contact NAR staff, and learn a myriad of vital information. NAR is also ultimately responsible for the awarding and assigning of designations and is involved in a series of partnerships with other entities, all evolving in the on-going interest of the professional REALTOR® (NAR actually owns the trademark on the term "REALTOR®").

Just as the State and Local Associations hold special events, the National Association will woo you with its outstanding once-a-year convention. Gigantic in size, vendors and affiliates from all over the country will fill up the many rows of booths, all bursting with real estate-related products and services. Here you can listen to fascinating keynote speakers, attend vital seminars, network with other REALTORS® and leadership from across the country. NAR will hold this annual event in different parts of the country each year, making it possible for every REALTOR® to attend , at least occasionally. One year it may be in Florida, then the next California. At any rate, do make it a priority to attend this event whenever you can—you won't be sorry!

National Volunteer Leadership

As we've already noted, volunteer leadership is an incredibly time-consuming responsibility. The local and state volunteer leadership includes many REALTORS® and represents members from each county and state. There is only one National President.

This elected official represents, supports, and works hard for the well being of REALTORS® in each and every state…not an easy task. This position clearly includes not only extensive responsibility, but it also involves an abundant amount of power. Usually, State leaders interested in running for NAR Presidency will start their campaign efforts years in advance.

Take the time to listen to the issues, concerns, and commitments that the presidential candidates are making. The person elected to office will play a large part in the direction of the industry and the way you do business, regardless of where you live (or sell).

Interview With the President

Richard A. Mendenhall, CCIM, CIPS, CRB, GRI

RE/MAX Boone Realty, Columbia Missouri- Owner/130+ REALTORS

Years in Business: 27

Presidency:

Columbia Board of REALTORS, 400 members, 1980

Missouri Association of REALTORS, 17,000 members, 1988

National Association of REALTORS, 750,000 members, 2001

Richard Mendenhall comes from five generations of real estate professionals. His mother and father were both active in their local, state, and national associations. While his parents certainly encouraged Richard to take the same interest in industry-related events, he acknowledges that his initial involvement was generally focused upon the excellent information he obtained when attending events.

"I felt that what was happening at the meetings I attended at the local, state, and, national level, was giving me ideas for a competitive edge in my market back home. I never, at any level, asked for any position. Someone always just asked me to serve in a certain capacity and I did it. This continued to happen, and ultimately, I was asked to run for State President, then National President. It was not a long term goal to do either."

When asked how he would explain to newcomer REALTORS® how important it is to become involved with their local, state, and national associations, here is what he said:

"It accelerates the agent's ability to know more about the industry and give them competitive edges, especially in knowing the changes that are coming so that they might prepare for them. Involvement also develops personal satisfaction, communications, and leadership skills."

Mr. Mendenhall also offered some unique advice on another reason REALTORS® can be proud:

"In just 92 years, REALTORS® have brought us the idealism, the vision, and the wisdom to create the most extraordinary and empowering system of property ownership the world has ever seen."

Richard Mendenhall has an exceptional outlook and extensive understanding of the real estate industry. His enthusiastic ability to combine his personal and professional beliefs in a manner that serves the industry so effectively is an inspiration to all REALTORS®, and one that should be modeled. Mr. Mendenhall offers various additional comments in later chapters.

By now, you have undoubtedly become more familiar with, and recognize the importance of, community and professional involvement. Hopefully, you can now see why such involvement is critical to your success. Yes, many people can pass a test and earn a license, but only those with the foresight and knowledge to join the ranks of the prestigious can call themselves REALTORS®.

> *Professional Profile*
>
> Judy McConville
> JudieMc@net.com
> Prudential McConville Realty, Ottawa, Illinois
> Years in Business: 25
>
> **"Amateurs are not respected in this business- you must develop
> strong relationships within your community, get involved with the
> local board, and understand the culture. A professional
> REALTOR® has standing in the community."**

The worksheet that follows will help you to document your records in organized real estate. Keep track of your membership number, as this will help identify you at all three levels of association involvement.

Also, note the dates of volunteer events or leadership posts you might hold. These will come in handy for resumes and bios you might need later on.

Finally, it is always a good idea to have your association contact information somewhere that is easy to access. Use this space to jot down names and numbers of those people you come into contact with at the local, state, and national level of organized real estate.

Use the worksheet on the following page to document your association membership records, volunteer roles, and association contacts. Anytime you serve in volunteer role, you should record it. It is the perfect addition to a resume or a marketing piece you are sharing with your prospective clients.

REALTOR® ASSOCIATION Membership & Community Involvement

Membership Number:_____Date:_____
Local Association   State Association   National Association

Volunteer Roles:
Date   Activity or Event

_____
_____
_____
_____
_____
_____
_____
_____
_____
_____

Association Contact Information:

_____
_____
_____
_____
_____
_____
_____
_____
_____
_____
_____
_____

Notes (annual events/trade shows/tech fairs/golf tournaments)

_____

_____

_____

_____

_____

_____

_____

_____

_____

_____

_____

_____

Time Management

"There are a million ways to lose a work day, but not even a single way to get one back."

Tom DeMarco and Timothy Lister

Nearly everyone has heard the expression before that tells us we all have the same twenty-fours hours in each day. Unfortunately, not everyone understands the most effective way to use them. When entering the business of real estate sales, time-management issues should be addressed right up front. Ask any successful REALTOR®, and they won't hesitate to tell you that time-management skills are as serious as commission checks, for without effective time-management skills, there will be no commission checks.

Many top producers have learned only through experience what type of time-management plan works best for them. What works for one successful REALTOR®, might be a disaster for another. This is why it is essential that each professional consider his or her own preferences, practices, and work history when developing a schedule. One thousand REALTORS® might each offer a different way to plan a working day, but none would disagree with the main point:

You must plan your work and work your plan

While most established agents and top producers have successful systems well in place, REALTORS® newer to the business still struggle in the all-important planning phase. At the end of this chapter we will consider an easy-to-alter workday plan that can assist you in your efforts to create a plan for success.

Professional Profile

Connie Miller

ConnieMiller@hotmail.com

ERA Mason Dixon Realty, DE

Years in Business: 13

"Always use a planner or some kind of Day timer…schedule everything, from family appointments to vacations, to all of your business appointments."

Tools of the Time Management Trade

REALTORS® across the continent agreed that they would be completely lost without some kind of scheduling tool. Some top producers rely on a laptop or palm pilot, while many others prefer the traditional hard-copy calendar, day timer, or note pad. Almost everyone maintains some kind of a "to-do" list. One top-producing agent in Colorado confided that she used a pile of spiral-bound notebooks to record voice mail messages, appointments, and birthdays.

There are plenty of options. The point is to experiment and discover which kind of tool works best for you, and then use it…faithfully. Even the smallest of tasks can be forgotten, particularly when the market is hot and the focus is on selling houses and closing escrows. The real estate industry presents numerous scheduling conflicts and challenges and any successful REALTOR® will concur that if they didn't control their schedule, it would most certainly control them!

Family Time, Family Support

One question that always comes up is "what about family time?" Obviously, working in the real estate industry can be quite conducive to working at least one day during the weekend, and perhaps both days when REALTORS are first getting established. Unlike many other professions, real estate activity often occurs when what corporate America considers "off time." The reason for this is simple. Think about your own experiences in buying or selling a home. Although, exceptions do exist.

Professional Profile

Cindy Kresi

kruesi@johnrwood.com

John R. Woods, Incorporated, Naples, Florida

Years in Business: 25

"I very rarely work in the evenings. Most people are happy to work with me during "normal" business hours. I schedule time off and I work smart."

Most people, logically enough, prefer to house hunt on the weekends, when they have the most amount of time and don't feel rushed. Many people would just as soon list their properties on the weekend or after they get off of work. And, since REALTORS® need to be accommodating to their clients, it is not unreasonable to expect to spend some of your evenings and weekends working with them. Since most families consider weekend time "family time," your own family may be affected. Most REALTORS® acknowledged that family and other personal relationships certainly may suffer if not dealt with appropriately.

Speaking of families, it's interesting to note how many "real estate families" exist in this country. There appear to be second and now, even third generation real estate professionals springing up everywhere (Remember President Mendenhall is a fifth generation REALTOR®). It's not at all unusual these days to find partners, spouses or parent/child working as a team. If this is something that sounds interesting to you, it is a wonderful way to spend quality time with family, while getting the job done in an effective manner. Regardless of whether anyone else in the family practices real estate, however, is not the point. Instead, it is to consider that if even one person in the house has committed to becoming a successful REALTOR®, the rest of the members of the household are going to have to offer support and understanding. It can be a very stressful job and dozens of top producers interviewed said they could never do what they do if they didn't have someone at home supporting their efforts one hundred percent.

Professional Profile

Celine Teeson, CBR,GRI

Celineteeson@REALTOR.com

Teeson Real Estate, South Burlington, Vermont

Years in Business: 25

"My husband and I are both very active REALTORS®. I was president of the Vermont Association of REALTORS® in 2000 and this has given me the opportunity to give back to a profession that has provided us with a great lifestyle. We attend NAR conventions yearly and then stay a few extra days for personal time. And there is another big reward about being married to someone in the business…we never lack conversation!"

> *Professional Profile*
>
> Nancy Hunt
>
> Nancy@nancyhunt.com
>
> RE/MAX Real Estate Services, San Clemente, California
>
> Years in Business: 23
>
> **"My husband and one son and one daughter are also in the business so the stress of working around unexpected appointments becomes a bit easier. My advice to others is to treat your personal life as an appointment, even though it might be just time spent with the family. This is something that clients will understand- they have families too."**

Still, there are times when the business can cause a conflict at home. Hundreds of established REALTORS® confirmed that the way they handle this dilemma is to schedule family time as if it were any other kind of appointment. Whether it's a child's birthday or a day spent with a spouse, it's critical that this time is allotted for as if it were a legitimate appointment…because it is. One REALTOR® in Texas told us she has a standing date with her husband that she keeps on her calendar and refuses to schedule anything else on that special day of the week. Also, include private time scheduled just for you.

In addition to time with family, it is important to schedule personal time. Whether it is a hobby or time spent socially, personal time is deemed crucial to making professional time more productive. Clearly, when the market is busy personal time feels like a distant dream, but try to schedule in periodic "play breaks," as a way of reward and self-rejuvenation. Also, this kind of time can be used to reassess your focus and ensure that you're heading your professional efforts in the right direction.

It is important to determine your professional goals and then work backward from that point, identifying what will be required to reach the level of success you have chosen.

Professional Profile

Carl E. Spencer
Carl@hgea.org
Hilo Brokers, Ltd. Hilo,
Years in Business: 9

"Set priority levels. When you're new, you feel you have to drop everything to try to generate a sale. People understand that sometimes you can't do things at the exact moment they want you to. You can have a personal life too, but you might have to sacrifice some income. So, know how high you want to go and then commit."

What About Assistants?

The idea of hiring an assistant seems to reveal some controversy, which in this business indicates that there are two sides to consider. There are many top producers who hold that their competently-qualified and usually licensed assistants are their saving grace, while others eschew the idea of hiring a personal assistant.

Professional Profile

Eric Howlett

Ehowlett@psre.com

Patterson-Schwartz, Dover, Delaware

Years in Business: 15

"First of all, if you're busy, you need to consider an assistant, otherwise you have no personal life at all. About 70% of my business, which is new construction, calls for weekend open houses. I try to take off every Thursday and arrange vacations during the week when the beach is less crowded!"

Professional Profile

Michael Keefrider
Keefrider@Keefrider.com
RE/MAX Premier, Albany, New York
Years in Business: 20

"My business has recently EXPLODED and with today's consumer needs, working with assistants and "teaming" is essential. As a successful agent today, you must be a good prospector, very proficient with technology, an outstanding communicator, and someone who places a high value on team building and making each client feel like they are your only client. Any agent today who does not have an assistant will not likely have a chance of growing his or her business. My staff has enabled me to grow because of their great help. Assistants are an enormous help to developing consumer confidence and facilitating one's ability to focus on providing outstanding service."

The positive aspect of assistants is that it gives REALTORS® more time to prospect, and more prospecting power. Imagine how convenient it is to have someone else sending out promotional mailings so that more time can be spent writing offers! On the other hand, some REALTORS® feel like they provide a better-quality service by keeping their work to themselves or perhaps investing in some part-time support with an escrow assistant. Again, this is an area that only personal preference can dictate. Obviously, new agents will most likely have no need to hire a personal assistant. However, once surrounded by accepted offers and active transactions in escrow, the determination will have to be made as to the most effective way to increase the business, or, to simply maintain it at a place that feels comfortable.

Keep in mind however, when it comes to hiring a personal assistant that you, as an employer, enter an entirely new arena that requires a significant amount of research concerning liability and taxes that should be carefully considered by qualified professionals, such as attorneys and accountants, for example.

Business Plans

Most top-producing REALTORS® will acknowledge the fact that in order to be a success, there has to be a plan. More simply put, it takes a map to get from point A to point B. Planning your business, your goals, and your marketing will automatically put you one step above those who fail to do so.

It's amazing how many new agents jump into the real estate business without a clue as to where they're going. It is crucial to establish a plan; make a map. Sit down and determine the direction you'll need to take to get to the place you want to be. Initially, a six-month and one-year goal should serve to get you started. Follow this up with long-term goals. Create annual plans as well as benchmark successes; five-year and ten-year goals. Identifying goals is an important part of success in the real estate industry and most accomplished REALTORS® would no more go forward without a plan than they would show up at a listing appointment without a contract.

Determining a career plan should be no different than any other kind of business plan. There are many effective books available, if additional direction is desired, but simply put, create end goals and then work backward to achieve them.

In order to sell 24 houses per year, determine how many will need to be sold each month (2) and then determine each task that will need to be performed in order to accomplish this goal. Say for example that one month you don't sell any houses, all is not lost. You will need to work twice as smart in the remaining months to compensate and even out the difference.

While shooting high is always an admirable trait, newcomers in the real estate business should recognize that there is a definite learning curve. Also, it's important to understand that nary a top producer became established over night. As a matter of fact, many of the top producers in this country live on referrals and repeat business.

Clearly, it takes time to establish a big enough client base so there is no need to go out and search for new business. When creating a business plan, aim high and shoot for success. Many experts agree that when developing a business plan, not only one-year, but also five-year, and maybe even longer, goals are needed. Write your goals down so that you can see them on paper. Writing a five-year goal now doesn't mean it's not subject to change over the next year to reflect a possible shift in direction. However, recent research that involved following college students who wrote their goals down, as well as fellow students who did not, revealed that those who had taken the time and energy to put their goals on paper were producing higher incomes and in general, leading happier lives.

It's clearly more effective to put your plan on paper. Somehow it brings a sense of validity to your goals and documents your intention to succeed. Get writing!

> *Professional Profile*
> Audrey Johnson
> AmJohnso@frontiernet.net
> Prudential Rochester Realty, Pittsford, New York
> Years in Business: 19
>
> **"Always plan your day the night before. This way, when you wake up, you will remember that you are employed and that you have a job to do. Real estate sales must be considered as any other professional career."**

The First Year

In most cases, the first year spent in real estate is time spent getting established. That is not to say that some level of income will not be generated, but rather, that making money is a by-product of becoming established in what is a highly competitive industry. Recognize this first year as a time of self-promotion, client-base building, and learning the ropes.

> *Professional Profile*
> Carolyn Cornelius
> CarolynCornelius@tyler.net
> Cathy Shipp and Associates Realty, Tyler, Texas
> Years in Business: 13
> **"Set aside time for paperwork and returning phone calls. I usually do this in the morning and spend the rest of the day committed to listings and sales."**

Upon entering the real estate industry, it is important to spend time understanding how the business operates. Scheduling classes, talking to top producers, and attending local, state, and national conventions are all excellent ways to become acclimated to the industry environment. In addition, these kinds of events enable serious REALTORS® to simultaneously get their faces and names "out there," networking with other like-minded real estate professionals.

When first becoming established in the business, it may not seem necessary to create a schedule, particularly when there are no appointments to fill it up with. This however, is simply not true. While standard appointments with others are easy to record and perhaps remember, it is those activities for which we are *not* accountable that are often the most difficult to complete. Let's repeat that:

It is those appointments for which we are not accountable that are often the most difficult to complete.

One successful RE/MAX REALTOR® admitted that scheduling time for "cold-calling" was the most challenging thing for her to do. "I just could never get up the nerve to go knocking on people's door." It is easy to become distracted from a task that we are not necessarily looking forward to. Even more so, when that task is self-imposed and not subject to outside verification. It's not your broker's job to ask you if you've marketed your area this week. Add to that challenge, the fact that many people are uncomfortable soliciting themselves to strangers. This is precisely why every REALTOR® should become adamant about creating a daily schedule or to-do list, and then stick to it!

Professional Profile

Eileen Patterson

Eileenpat@earthlink.com

Shear, Hesperia,

Years in Business: 22

"Have a routine and stick to it! Whatever you do, remember to continue farming and working leads, even when you think you don't have time- this way you'll still have something to turn to when the escrow closes."

The schedule that follows may be altered, added to, deleted from, or completely revamped. The purpose of this example is to demonstrate the importance of creating a daily schedule and then sticking to it. Success will only be achieved when a business plan is implemented and then broken down into daily tasks. This schedule has been designed for the new agent who has not yet established any leads nor opened any escrows and basically provides but one idea of how working hours can be allotted to positively promote a growing business.

8:30 a.m. Arrive at office, check messages, return calls if applicable
Spend morning checking **FSBO** listings, creating marketing pieces, networking. (FSBBO=For Sale By Owners homes found in real estate classified or on-line)
Spend the afternoon visiting **farm** area. (Farm Area=The particular area or neighborhood an agent tries to become an established expert in)
Let the other agents in the office know you are more than willing to take their "**floor time**" and hold their listings "**open**." (Floor Time=to answer random telephone calls –"ad calls," that may lead to potential clients) (Open=hosting an Open House so that potential buyers may come and view listed properties)
Spend time creating relationships with affiliates
Spend time modeling top producers with admirable track records
Continue networking until a pre-set number of contacts have been made

Many REALTORS® acknowledge that when they are first starting out, they will strive for a specific number of calls each day. Since generating leads is the primary method of getting things rolling, meeting your daily quota will be key.

Keep in mind that once the first lead has been established, the entire picture will change. Also keep in mind that the first lead can be established immediately. In order to follow up on a lead, time will be spent searching out properties through MLS, setting up appointments with buyers, other agents, and homeowners and tenants to show listings. For listing leads, time will be spent searching for "comps" and preparing the listing presentation. The expression "building a business" is very accurate in the real estate industry. It is not unlike building a house, one brick at a time.

In order to better understand how the daily schedule or "to do" list of an agent with active listings, open escrows, and potential buyers, dramatically changes, consider the following schedule that is focused upon success:

Morning: Check messages, return calls promptly, set up appointments with home inspector at a time convenient for seller Schedule appointment to show Mr. Buyer new properties over the weekend
Update transaction folder with new loan info and call escrow officer
Check MLS for new listings for Mr. Buyer Check MLS for new sales or listing in Ms. Seller's neighborhood for comparisons
Make appointments with homeowners or tenants to show Mr. Buyer properties
Send out "Just Listed" cards to Ms. Seller's area
Check in with Ms. Seller, ensuring that sale sign and lock box have been put up and report any progress/leads/feedback on listing
Check in with Lender for Mr. Buyer's qualifications, double check on Ms. Seller's escrow status
Call on at least ten "For Sale By Owners" or expired listings
Cover Floor time from 4-6 p.m.

The schedule above clearly indicates that once leads, listings, and escrow accounts have begun, the day will fill up rapidly. It is these sometimes seemingly small tasks that are critical however, to the long-term success of any REALTOR®. This is why it is crucial that each day has been organized in a manner that is conducive to accomplishing the tasks at hand while simultaneously taking steps to ensure increased sales opportunities.

Luanna Vaughn, a busy REALTOR® in Carmichael, California, had some insightful thoughts to share on the importance of time management.

"I return phone calls promptly and keep scheduled appointments. I never overbook, because when you overbook, you're always rushed and stand a much greater chance of being late for an appointment. Punctuality is a must in this business-I'm *always* on time."

"The key is to be flexible. In this business, your priorities can change at the drop of a dime, and you've got to be prepared for anything, at anytime."

That is such a valid and important statement, that it would do many REALTORS® well to post it in a obvious location as a constant reminder that, in this industry, change is the name of the game. This is why it is so important to keep a close account of those things you *are* able to control, because there will be plenty of issues that are *not* within your control. "Surprises" are difficult enough to contend with, let alone allowing the rest of your business to fall apart from lack of planning.

Virtually any new REALTOR® can glean insight from the intelligent tidbits provided from the experienced and successful REALTORS® interviewed here. And, it is undoubtedly true, that literally thousands of professional top producers acknowledge effective time management skills as being vital to continued success.

In summary, time is what you make it. It can be your enemy or your best friend. The crucial component is *planning, planning, planning*. Plan your appointments, plan your day, and plan your day off. Simple things like delivering an offer might not seem important enough to deserve a place in your appointment book. However, if it's something that you might forget, or that requires even ten minutes of your time…it's worth writing down and remembering.

Putting your goals on paper is an effort you'll want to make upon entering the real estate sales arena. With high-level competition and a multitude of distractions, staying focused on your monthly, annual, and end goals will be an integral component to your success. Write it down!

Use the following pages to your advantage by making them a permanent part of your business. In addition, don't forget to invest in a good daily/weekly/monthly calendar that will give you plenty of room to note all of your tasks. Make lists, write goals, and sell loads of real estate!

BUSINESS PLAN

ONE YEAR Date:_____ (to check back)

# Houses Sold	Projected	Actual

Gross Sales/Net Sales

_____
_____
_____

Other One Year Goals:

_____
_____
_____
_____
_____
_____

_____

_____

_____

FIVE YEAR Date:_____(to check back)

Houses Sold	Projected	Actual

_____

_____

Gross Sales/Net Sales

_____

_____

_____

Other Five Year Goals:

_____

_____

_____

_____

_____

_____

_____

Marketing & Understanding The Market

"Success usually comes to those who are too busy to be looking for it"

David Henry Thoreau (1817-1862)

There are many effective marketing strategies that you can employ to help you become more successful in real estate sales. The main point of marketing in this industry, however, is to present your name to prospective clients so that a source of referrals can be set in place and new business opportunities established. So, while there are many effective marketing techniques that are both traditional as well as more contemporary, the main point to remember about real estate marketing is this:

You are promoting yourself to the public so that your name and your face will become known and associated with successful real estate trans-actions-usually in a particular area or specialty

FSBO

A "FSBO" is a house that is For Sale By Owner. Statistics show that most individuals who decide to try and sell their own home, usually end up hiring a REALTOR® once they realize what an enormous amount of work and potential risk it really involves. Keep in mind that this technique is as old as the hills and the moment that a "For Sale by Owner" sign hits the ground, several dozen real estate sales people will most likely answer to the call. The challenge then, is to present yourself uniquely and professionally in a manner that makes you stand out from the crowd. Here is where style of salesmanship will come into play. Remember though, that there are many agents who will contact the homeowners, eager to get the listing. While it may be tempting, here is as good a case as any to reiterate the importance of ethics in communications.

Don't promise anything you can't deliver

Open Houses

Many REALTORS® dread open houses. There is a tentative belief in this industry that the only thing open houses are usually good for is picking up new buyers, not selling the listing. And while that's certainly not always the case, chances are that many listing agents would concur. Even if open houses don't always sell houses, trying to explain that to a seller seldom, if ever, works. This puts the new or not so busy agent in an ideal situation.

When first becoming established in the business, speed up the process a bit by volunteering to hold other REALTOR'S® (who are in your office) listings open. The incentive for the listing agent is 1) it makes the listing agent's sellers very happy sellers, and; 2) you never know…it just might sell. The incentive for you is: 1) the newer agent stands to make many contacts with potential buyers, and; 2) you never know…it just might sell, and; also, it does newer agents well to endear themselves to other, established agents.

One caveat about holding other agent's listings as open houses: the other agent must be from your firm! A REALTOR® from Prudential would not hold open a listing for another agent from Century 21. So check with the established and busy agents in your office, determine who has listings in your farm area, and volunteer to help them out.

Farm Area

Essentially, there are two choices. You can take any open houses and call upon any FSBOs (For Sale By Owner) you know of, or you can concentrate on your "farm" area. Historically, agents have worked it both ways, but more often than not, focused upon one or two particular areas. The specific area that the REALTOR® selects is where she will invest her advertising dollars and "door to door " efforts. A farm area is generally a particular neighborhood or region, maybe even a whole town. Naturally, times are changing and with the advent of technology and increased transportation, more REALTORS® seem to be less concerned with particular farm areas. That is not to say however, that "farming" is not alive and well in the real estate industry.

Professional Profile

Carole de Losda, LTG,RRC, WCR 2001 President
Carole@besthomeREALTOR.com
Century 21 SCVA, Campbell, California
Years in Business: 10

"I love to walk my farm area and even if you use direct mail, you need to make a personal visit every quarter. I always leave something permanent with a picture on it so they won't forget who to call when they need a REALTOR®."

Many successful agents farm more than one area. They may travel door to door or simply farm an area by sending out consistent mailings.

Direct Mailings

Entire books have been written (and are referenced in the back) on effective mailings and telephone marketing techniques for REALTORS®. Basically however, sending out "Just Listed" postcards, letters, or door hangers, further increase the likelihood of potential sales contacts. The "Just Listed" advertising informs homeowners in the area that one of their neighbors has just listed a home with you. Often, the same thing is done to invite homeowners (or renters) in the neighborhood to open houses. Once the property is sold, sending out "Just Sold" cards reminds the homeowners in the area of who you are and what you just accomplished.

The "Just Sold" advertising is very effective because now you have proven to the neighborhood what a competent job of selling homes you do.

Often times, with "Just Listed" advertising, curious neighbors will telephone in an attempt to find out what price their neighbor and REALTOR® expects to bring in for the property. Even if the effort is merely a curious one, it is still an ideal opportunity for the listing agent to establish some kind of rapport with the caller.

Sending "Just Listed" and "Just Sold" announcements, will help lend credibility to your skills and help get you established as a *reliable* REALTOR® in that particular neighborhood.

Rule number one of real estate marketing is:

Everyone is a potential client

Some REALTORS® report sending out monthly newsletter, flyers, and brochures. Marketing can certainly be a costly endeavor, especially when considering the rate of return, which is relatively low. Fortunately, however, the more marketing material that is sent out, the better the chances of getting a lead. When first starting out in the business, every lead counts, and leads will come from the most unexpected places. That doesn't mean you won't have to put an earnest effort into getting the ball rolling. It is crucial to invest in self-promotion, and it helps to remember that marketing expenses are tax-deductible.

Professional Profile

Richard Henk
DickHenk@sundragon.net
D & K Henk Realty, Incorporated, Florida
Years in Business: 12

"I list 120 to 135 properties per year (I list and my wife sells). I try to average 200 to 300 postcards a week to subdivisions in our town. We send each and every month a newsletter to all of our listings and leads kept in our Top Producer database. We have offered free market analysis for 12 years and carry an average of 70 to 75 active listings."

Promotion, Promotion, Promotion

Promotion really is the name of the game. The more your name is out there, the more quickly it comes to mind when someone is ready to buy or list a property. In addition to direct mailing, remember to think outside of the box. Think about advertising on local television, radio, bus and park benches, storefront windows, billboards, and flyers to other agents. There are a number of ways you can promote yourself. In addition to direct mailings, remember to:

- Always carry business cards and distribute them to everyone you meet.
- Hold "Home Buyer Seminars" to drum up buyer business.
- Always, *always,* follow up with past clients (send holiday cards, birthday greetings, or your personalized newsletter).
- Wear "REALTOR®" or Company branded apparel/hats/bags to be a "walking advertisement."
- Send personal notes to people in the local community (congratulations on your wedding, promotion, birth, etc.).

- "Rent" unique advertising space, such as park or bus stop benches, mini-bill boards, web sites, local newspapers, and relevant trade publications.
- Attend every local, state, and national trade show or conference you can and network, network, network.
- Invest in professionally printed brochures that will help to promote your talent/experience/skill, area of specialization, and of course, designations.
- Attend local MLS meetings and "pitch" your listings to other agents.
- Invest in flyer distribution services for both promoting yourself (to neighborhoods, in parking lots, apartment complexes, etc.) and for promoting your property listings to other agents in various offices.
- Be available. All the advertising in the world can't begin to pay off if you're not easily accessible (work, home, and cell numbers, as well as email address and website URL should be bright, bold, and easy to find on your business cards, flyers, brochures, and advertisements).
- Have "REALTOR®" printed on your checks, following your name.

Electronic Advertising

Under the technology chapter, we will go into greater detail with online marketing opportunities. But for right now, it is important to remember that email lists and client contacts can all be made electronically. Also, web sites that offer images of listed properties are an excellent way to pick up potential clients. As more and more consumers are becoming reliant on the instantaneous answers the Internet can provide, the more provocative and promotional tool it is becoming, and will continue to be.

Referral Fees

Another common practice among professional REALTORS® is the act of referral fees. This is not a "charge" but rather a "gift" that an agent might offer another agent, once a referred transaction has closed escrow. Many REALTORS® advertise this on the back of their business cards or in magazines that they are buying ad-space from. Often times an agent will have an opportunity to list a property which is located outside of her area and too far for her to do an effective job of selling it. It is common in these instances for the REALTOR® to call or look for another REAL-TOR® who is closer to the area in question and "refer" them the business. The cordial and correct thing to then do, once the property has been sold, the escrow closed, and the commission paid, is for agent "B" to give agent "A" an agreed upon referral fee.

Professional Profile

Carl Phillips
Prudential, Massachusetts
Years is Business: 20

"Referral fees are a great way to motivate other agents and clients to keep sending buyers my way."

Referrals are certainly a wonderful way to acquire and increase your business. Make it a point to let the world know you appreciate referral business, and remember in turn, to show that appreciation.

Professional Profile

Beth Robertson
Byrlst8@aol.com
Prudential California, Sonoma, California
Years is Business: 32

"I work every day, literally. I get out there and network in the community dealing with different groups, working with the local association. I have a good rapport with a relocation company and alignment with school boards. All of this is so that I am established as a trusted professional in my area. This is how I earn my referral business."

Word of mouth is certainly an established way for many successful REALTORS® to procure referral business. Networking and socializing can have a tremendous impact on becoming known as the REALTOR® to call, in any particular circle or area.

So keep in mind that the earlier portion covering community involvement also serves to support one of the most effective means of self-promotion available to REALTORS® everywhere…get involved in the community, get your face and name known to the neighborhood, and sell houses!

Ultimately, everything you do in this business affects your long-term success. Those REALTORS® who keep current on real estate issues, stay involved within their community, promote themselves, and then follow up that promotion with honest ethical, dealings and communications, are those REALTORS® who will enjoy the rewards of continuous, repeat, and referral business. In a nutshell, that's what this business is all about.

MARKETING

Check List of Promotional Items to Have on Hand
Business Cards-*always, always, always*
Self-promoting Brochures
Flyers for Active Listings
Testimonials or Letters of Recommendation from past clients

Farm Area:_____Map Coordinates_____

_____

Farming/Marketing Activities Planned:

_____
_____
_____
_____
_____
_____
_____
_____
_____
_____

Advertising Rates:

Publication	Cost	Telephone/email

_____
_____
_____
_____

Designers/Printers	Name	Contact Information

MARKETING SCRIPTS & TIPS

Ad Calls-Remember to ask qualifying questions. When possible, open-ended questions work best. Following are some examples of good ad call lead-in questions:

- Are you working with another agent?
- Have you been pre-qualified?
- What price range are you looking in?
- What kind of monthly payment are you considering?
- Approximately what kind of down payment were you thinking about?

- Do you own your own home now and would you need to sell it first?
- How long have you been looking?
- What neighborhood are you most interested in?
- Who will be living in the house?
- What are the most important features you are looking for?

Additional Questions you find useful:

_____

_____

_____

_____

_____

_____

_____

_____

Naturally, you won't want to shoot these questions out all in succession, but the more you can find out about prospective buyers, the better off you are in helping them to find the home they are seeking. Most of all, remember that many ad callers never end up buying the home they call on, but rather another home that the agent was able to find for them, because the agent new the right questions to ask.

Successful ad calls end in appointments. Don't forget the careful telephone close, such as:

When would you like to see it?
Is tomorrow good, or would you prefer next week?

Add your own:

_____

_____

_____

_____

NOTE: Always get names and phone numbers of ad callers and confirm prior to appointment. People who have given their contact information are less likely to stand you up.

In real estate sales, you'll be writing lots of follow up letters and thank you notes that should always be timely and heartfelt. Beyond that, you'll be doing additional writing that will truly represent you or the property you are promoting.

What follows are three sample scripts for marketing letters that work. Please feel free to use these, altering them so that they reflect the property, neighborhood, price range, etcetera, specific to the situation.

For Sale By Owner:

Dear Mr. Seller,

Congratulations on your decision to sell your home!

As a specialist working in your neighborhood, I'm happy to let you know that the most recently closed transaction on your street sold for $145,000. This comparative market analysis should help you to determine the current value of your home-although it is only a starting point, and one of many factors.

Because your neighborhood is important to me, I'd like to offer my support. Selling your own home is big step, and you can use all the expert advice available. If you would like to set up a time to get a better feel for whether or not your home has been priced accordingly, just give me a call.

I wish you all the best in your home-selling endeavor!

Sincerely,

Your name

Here we have done what is known as a "soft sell." That is not to say that sometimes a harder sell is not appropriate or warranted, but rather, people who have decided to sell their own home are generally trying to save money, and are tired of dozens of agents who have called them and asked for the listing. You've introduced yourself in a very low-pressure manner, which people seem to respond well to. In addition, some agents go so far as including a neighborhood newsletter, home-selling tips, or some other "keeper" items that will endear the agent to the home-seller. The home-seller will remember the no-pressure REALTOR® who helped them out, and that's who they'll call when they know it's time to list the house.

Marketing Letter Buyers:

Dear Buyer (or renter):

Are you tired of throwing your money away?

Do you realize that what you're spending each month on rent could be easily applied to a home mortgage?

What are the benefits of owning a home?

- Financial investment that keeps growing
- Excellent tax advantages
- Pride of ownership

Owning a home has never been easier. There are many great loan programs now available that help first time buyers secure the home of their dreams. And here's the other good news: buyers never pay the commission, sellers do! That means it's never too soon to secure the services of a qualified REALTOR® for counseling on your home buying decision.

If you'd like to see how much you qualify for, contact me at your convenience and I'll arrange for an absolutely free consultation.

Isn't it time your start investing in yourself?

Sincerely,

Your name

Generally speaking, benefits for first time buyers are easy to assess and are noted in the brief letter above. When you are marketing buyers who are not buying their first home, the benefits are the same, although they will most likely already be aware of them.

Another approach for buyers who have already owned a home might be very different than the letter above, which is primarily targeted at first-time buyers. If you are marketing someone who is already a homeowner, but perhaps is looking to invest or buy up into another home, be sure to use a tone that doesn't imply they've never owned a home before.

Marketing Letter Sellers:

Dear Homeowner:

As a professional REALTOR® who is committed to success-fully selling homes in your neighborhood, I wanted to take this opportunity to introduce myself.

If you have ever considered selling your current home, buying another, or are just curious to know what your property is worth, please call me. I would be happy to set up a time to view your home and tell you about the recent sales in your neighborhood.

Looking forward to assisting you in your real estate endeavors.

Sincerely,

Your Name

Essentially, the marketing materials aimed at sellers and buy-ers should be direct and serve to promote your individual skills and success. Some agents who send frequent marketing letters to their farm area include resumes, newsletters, or other items the homeowners are sure to retain, or at least read over.

With any marketing material, remember that you are repre-senting yourself to your public. Ensure that spelling, grammar, and tone are pleasing and appropriate.

Advertisements

There are wonderful books available that will assist you in writing effective marketing letters and real estate advertisements. Here though, we will briefly consider some of the key considerations in writing effective ad copy that sells. Remember, that while smart marketing is honored in the industry, honesty is first and foremost. Don't say something in your ad that is simply not true, or you will earn a reputation as an unethical agent. Most buyers will note that things that seem too good to be true usually are, and other agents won't want to show your listings.

Abbreviations

In newspaper ads, you are charged by the word, and often only allotted a small amount of space. It is therefore vital that you learn to abbreviate in a manner that gets your point across, without confusing readers. Review your Sunday Classified section Real Estate section and become familiar with the accepted forms of abbreviations used in your region. Here are a few examples of some very basic abbreviations found in newspaper ads:

> BR=Bedroom
> 3/2= or any number set up as such, indicates # bedrooms and baths
> CH=Central heat or CH/A, CHA can all refer to central heat and air
> FIXER=A fixer-upper home-one that needs work
> FR=Family room

Copy Points

Remember that people buy benefits, not features. In real estate ads however, they want both. Don't spend too much time in poetic prose when shaping your ads. Instead, state the facts and opt for catching your readers' eye with headlines that shout benefits, copy that clarifies features.

- Great Investment! This 3/2,FR,.........
- Doll House! Cute 2/1, w/oak cabs.........
- Huge Lot! 3/2 built on .75 acr., barn.........
- Room to Grow! 4/2,FR,sep dining, near schools.........
- Fixer Upper! 3/1 desired area, needs roof
- Dream House! 3/2.5,new appliances
- Walk to Work! 2/1 shady downtown condo
- Great Pool! 3/2, den, blt-in pool
- Established Area! 2/2 cute floorplan
- Near Park! 3/2 nestled close to park
- Gourmet Kitchen! 3/1 w/huge kitchen

It is wise to spend some time developing the perfect ad. Have a standard collection that you can call upon and freshen up or alter to fit your current needs.

WHERE TO HANG YOUR LICENSE

"When people go to work, they shouldn't have to leave their hearts at home."
Betty Bender

Deciding which broker and firm will best suit your individual needs, particularly at first, is not unlike entering into holy wedlock. Yes, you can always move on, but please do not underestimate the important role broker selection plays in establishing yourself in the real estate industry. The masses of top producers are torn in their advice to new agents concerning broker size. There are many who proclaim big is better and then there are those who suggest small is safer, and then there are the literally thousands of firms that fall somewhere in between. While the ultimate choice should be a personal one that has been carefully weighed considering one's own standards and priorities, there are a number of factors, as well as opinions, that might serve to help those who are ready to take that first step. Here, we will explore the kinds of options and expectations you should be keeping in mind when selecting a place to hang your license.

Professional Profile

Sandy Beeler, ABR, CRS, GRI, LTG

Homes@sandybeeler.com

RE/MAX Preferred, Knoxville, Tennessee

Years in Business: 13

"Find a non-competing, educated, continually informed broker who is active on the city and, at least, the state level of leadership. One who stays up to dated on ALL the rules and has a real interest in his business and in yours."

What's a Broker For?

There are a few things about brokers you'll need to understand before we go any further into the wonders of the real estate world. Real estate sales people can only sell real estate if and when their license is placed with a licensed broker. Just because someone has taken the required courses, paid the fees, and passed the exam, does not mean that the individual can cavort around and start selling houses. Anyone who is already working in the real estate industry knows what a mess that would be!

A broker serves as the party who is accountable for his agent's actions. Whatever you as an agent do, can have an impact upon your broker. Needless to say, brokers assume much responsibility for those otherwise "independent contractors" that agents tend to be. Brokers must exercise, out of necessity, extreme caution when considering new agents into the office or firm. The next chapter deals exclusively with a broker's point of view, but let's concentrate first, on what kinds of things you'll want to think about when interviewing brokers.

Professional Profile
William Fryer
WmFryer@henderson.net
Fryer Appraisal, Henderson, Kentucky
Years in Business: 30

"New agents should find out how active the broker is in the day to day business and whether or not the broker is in the office most every day, or at least easily accessible."

Yes, you will definitely want to interview brokers just as they in turn, will want to interview you. The fit must be right. The opportunities and potential must promise to be mutually rewarding and fulfilling or else the relationship is a waste of time.

When talking to hundreds, if not thousands, of REALTORS® over a number of years, one thing becomes apparent. The broker makes a difference. The exact components of what that difference is, rests upon the REALTOR® making the selection. And, it is a highly personal and unique criterion indeed. While only you can determine your personal preferences and priorities, there is a particular group of issues that seem to be rather common in playing a vital role in broker selection.

While only you will know what ultimately works best for you, there are several factors that you will probably want to consider, and keep in mind, when interviewing potential brokers.

Professional Profile

Janet McKay

JanetMckay@yahoo.com

Long & Foster, Waldorf, MD

Years in Business: 3

"Not only should you ask a lot of questions when selecting a broker, but you should find out how he feels about getting a phone call on a Saturday evening- ask if he has a pager. When you're newer to the business like I am, you need to ensure constant support."

Joining the Team

A broker will not be, per se, like a corporate executive officer in his demands. You are an independent contractor. However, don't think for a minute that brokers never have to reprimand their agents. Also, don't fool yourself into thinking a broker cannot ask you to leave. A broker can. On the other side of the coin, brokers owe their agents a certain amount of direction, support, and recognition. Clearly then, a professional relationship must be affable for both you and the broker you are considering.

You needn't think that the broker you work for is the greatest person on the face of the earth. You must however, trust him as an individual, respect him, and be willing to join the firm as a committed team player. Many agents will place their license with the first broker they come across. The thinking is that real estate is a single-player game, but nothing could be further from the truth, as you will see.

Professional Profile

Kathie Frank, ABR, LTG
Kathi@kathiefrank.com
Keller Williams Realty, Conroe, Texas
Years in Business: 20

"The culture in the office should be supportive for individual growth."

One of the important factors of selecting a broker then, will be the broker's own style, philosophy, and, tactics, as well as, the atmosphere generated in the office between the other agents. Even if you plan to work from your "home office," as many REALTORS® do, you will still have to abide by your broker's strategies, policies, practices, and ethics, as well as, depend upon him when you have a problem, question, or unusual circumstance. Also, it is inevitable that the overall office environment will be a direct reflection on you and your business; other agents will show your listings and take your ad calls, secretaries will answer your calls, and the general office practices will be evident in your own work. Most offices hold weekly sales meetings too, and this is a prime time to share your own listings and hear about new ones in your office.

So the first step is to find a broker and an office that makes you feel good. A person and a place holding the potential to support and inspire you. First find a broker you can work with, one who you feel comfortable talking with, then let the negotiations begin.

Commission Splits/ Fees

Any REALTOR® will tell you, real estate is a money game. The earning potential is fabulous, and it all starts with the brokerage. There are two things to think about when considering broker negotiations; commission splits and fees.

Commission splits can vary significantly from one broker to the next, and generally this is due to the various other factors that figure into the overall equation. It is not uncommon for brokers to offer a kind of "escalating" split. In other words, say the commission split starts out at fifty percent for the broker, fifty percent for the agent (50-50), it might advance to a split that is more in the agent's favor, based upon production. Production doesn't just involve the number of transactions a particular agent has closed, but also the total dollar amount that those transactions have generated. Commission splits can be a tricky thing and it is in any new agent's best interest to discuss the topic thoroughly with the broker. Also, it doesn't hurt to confer with other established REALTORS® for feedback on the variances of commission splits.

While some brokers may offer commission splits that seem less than adequate, there are often fee-based considerations that must be taken into account too.

Professional Profile
Emil Mongeon
Emil@REALTOR.com
LEGACY Properties, Brentwood, Tennessee
Years in Business: 5

"Look at training first, then how the firm ranks in the community, and then comes commission splits...."

An example of this would be a broker who wants to keep half of the commission split, yet charges no desk, telephone, MLS, or E&O (Errors and Omissions Insurance) fees. Another broker may allow agents to keep most or all of the commission check, but then charge a monthly desk fee as high as $1,000.00. Of course, these are dramatically opposing examples and in reality, there are many scenarios that will fall somewhere in between.

Since there is no guarantee on how much commission a REALTOR® will earn each month, deciding which kind of option works best isn't always easy. Some months will be abundant, and then there will be those that are not. This is of special concern when first breaking into the business.

Since commission splits vary, as do individual office fees, it is important to take all factors into serious consideration before choosing. Many agents start out thinking the highest split must be the best, without realizing how quickly those office fees can add up. Furthermore, most established agents will advise those interested in breaking into the real estate industry to make sure they've got enough of a "stash," or another source of income, as those first few months can be brutal, income-wise.

Professional Profile

Penny Romito, WCR State Governor, E-Pro 500 Certified
Romitop@nwbedbreakfastinns.com
RE2k.Com, Tacoma, Washington
Years in Business: 22

"New agents should ask what is the compensation split and then find out about the costs that are associated with doing business in the office: franchise fees, B&O Taxes, L&I Insurance, E&O Insurance, use of copier, long distance calls, Real Estate signs, forms, and business cards."

There is more to commission splits and office fees than meets the eye. It is only through thorough examination, wise budget-planning, and inquisitive research that the new agent is able to determine the best choice for his or her personal preference.

Technology

Brokers in many states have jumped on the technology bandwagon. Some however, jump quicker and faster than others. If you are new to the real estate industry, let alone technology, it might be important for you to find a broker who is techno-savvy. A broker need not be the Internet King or understand computer programming. He should however, recognize technology as playing a vital and on-going role in the real estate industry.

Many brokers and office managers actually have hired technical staff on board. This is especially true in some franchises, where networked systems are the norm. Brokers who recognize the importance of technology also appreciate current trends and are, therefore, demonstrating an undeniable effort to stay alive in an ever-evolving industry. Even if you, as an agent, have no specific interest or ability in technology, it would be a wise choice to merge with a broker who does.

> *Professional Profile*
>
> Anna Paige Durant
> ApDurant@sc.rr.com
> Russell & Jeffcoat, Columbia, South Carolina
> Years is Business: 15
>
> "Besides broker reputation, types of continuing education, office atmosphere and morale, I would look at what type of equipment the firm is using. For example, how many computers, how quickly they work, Internet access, and technical support."

Many firms and offices have developed effective web sites, allowing their agents to post listings and establish email addresses. Technology is definitely an ongoing trend in the real estate industry. While it may not be the most important factor in selecting a broker to work with, the level of technology a firm works at, might be a definite indicator of how concerned the firm is with staying on top of the industry.

Reputation/Community Involvement

Selling real estate is an honorable profession. It is however, through the on-going effort of organized real estate, and local, state, and national associations, that real estate has developed into the noble industry that it is today. That is not to say however, that everyone in the real estate industry acts with honor.

Professional Profile

Diane Varni
Century 21 Stackhouse, Stafford, Virginia
Years in Business: 2
"New agents need to know their broker's standing in the local and state associations because brokers who are involved are also better informed and can work through conflicts more intelligently."

Generally speaking, any new REALTOR® should consider broker reputation and community involvement as an important criteria. If the broker you are interviewing with does not care whether you plan on joining the ranks of organized real estate, he may not be a broker you want to consider. Moreover, he himself should be involved, at least to some degree, in local or state real estate issues.

First of all, most brokers will insist you join the three levels of associations discussed earlier-it's not an option. A smart broker recognizes the value that organized real estate adds to his agent's ability, skill, knowledge, and industry awareness. That being the case, an efficient broker sets a good example. Perhaps it is only at a local level, maybe a committee of some kind, but an effective broker will demonstrate for his agents and his community that he is dedicated to the on-going efforts of professional improvement. A broker who remains educated and updated with important real estate issues, and especially one who plays a role in the outcome, is a broker you can count on to share the news with you.

As a general rule of thumb, actions speak louder than words. Therefore, most real estate firms must adhere to a strict professional standard, and when they don't, their reputation may be marred. Avoid interviewing with brokers who have acted with questionable honesty or ethics. Pay attention to the consumer reaction when a certain firm's name is mentioned. Remember, when you hang your license with a broker, you are hanging it with his firm. If you're not proud of the place you put your license, how do you expect to be effective in representing it?

Advertising/Promotion

Another consideration is advertising. Some brokers will pay to advertise your listing in the weekend classified section, some won't. There are firms that will provide you with all of the stock stationery and marketing materials you could ever ask for, and those who make you buy your own forms. Again, this is part of the overall program.

Don't reject a firm merely because they won't provide you with a stack of "Just Listed" postcards, but then again, keep that in mind when considering a firm that won't. Advertising assistance is just one of the several important components involved in weighing one firm against another. Keep in mind too, the impact the firm name plays in advertising. It's perfectly acceptable to create promotional material where you and your name are the predominant feature on the piece, whereas, company-produced marketing material will generally serve to advertise the firm's name more prominently.

Some well-known firms might sell themselves because most everyone has at least heard of them or seen their signs. This should be considered as an advertising perk for you, which might well compensate for the fact that they won't be picking up the tab for your new business cards.

While promotional pieces are important, most top producers would argue that ad space in the local newspaper is even more of an issue. Quite clearly, this kind of cost can add up, particularly if you have several listings at one time. This is also a good selling point when working with potential sellers; it's much easier to promise you will advertise the seller's property each weekend when you know that cost is not an issue.

Professional Profile

Peter Sulzbach

Sulzbach@frontiernet.net

RE/MAX Benchmark, Goshen, New York

Years in Business: 15

"While choosing a broker has to do with the current market and the REALTOR'S® individual needs and goals, technology has changed things so that networking and marketing can all be done electronically. So, size and marketing support don't matter as much as they used to."

Size

Is big better or small safer? The jury remains out on this particular issue. It is by no coincidence that this question can be answered either way, and for a number of reasons. Big offices have certain benefits that smaller offices lack, and smaller offices provide benefits that big offices might not. Like most other considerations in choosing a firm, the final decision will be based on your personal preferences. And, with careful research and prudent interviews, it's quite possible to find an office that fully meets or exceeds your greatest expectations. So how does the matter of size affect the new agents?

The first thing to understand about determining the importance of office size, is that no two offices will be exactly alike and that size isn't necessarily a solid gauge for choosing the office that you will feel most motivated in. There are however, two consistently supported points of view worth mentioning about big versus small.

Professional Profile

Scott Crum

Scottcrm@micron.net

Andy Enrico & Company, Boise, Idaho

Years in Business: 10

"I have always worked for a small broker- big offices have a lot of babysitting going on. Being a small office, we call the shots and we can be as flexible as we would like to be."

Professional Profile

Lyn Markham

LynJim1@aol.com

RE/MAX Select, Ashburn, Virginia

Years in Business: 12

"You must consider the education that larger firms often provide. I myself started at a smaller firm and received hands-on training, so it's really a toss up."

With a big office, particularly a well-known firm, your advertising is somewhat automatic. Many agents stated that they recommended newer agents become involved with a larger-sized firm because of the instantaneous name recognition. Large firms with many agents also have, presumably, many listings. Many listings make the phone ring, hence your time spent on the floor answering ad calls, might be greatly increased with a large firm. There will also be more agents to offer your open house sitting services to, and of course, more agents to pitch your listings to, once you've acquired an inventory. Also, bigger firms tend to have pre-printed stationery, forms, and a host of marketing materials to help you get established in your business.

Another big perk with a large office relates to the number of top producers you can observe and imitate, expediting your sales efforts. So what about the flip side?

Small to medium firms don't come without merit. An equally large number of top producers suggested that newer agents might want to get their feet wet with a firm that is small enough to provide more personalized training. All firms, regardless of size, offer REALTORS® some kind of training; avoid those that do not. The most frequently supported argument concerning the benefits of less than large firms (small to medium) was the atmosphere. A significant number of top producers acknowledged that smaller offices harbored more of a "family" atmosphere. As part of this comfortable community, agent assistance and guidance might be easier to come by and competition within the same office might not be as fierce. Another, less tangible but certainly noted remark about smaller and mid-sized firms, is that upper management was never far away; there were no "company policies" that filtered down from some distant locale.

Remember though, this is all relative. Size cannot be the only determining factor in dictating the overall office environment, nor can it be a valid measurement for how successful you will become. As previously stated, there is no "right" answer when it comes to office size. The best advice is simply to keep the pros and cons of office size tucked neatly in your notebook, and when the time comes, ask the broker, agents in the office, and yourself, "is this a good fit?"

Competing vs. Non-Competing

Most new agents aren't really clear on this concept and how it might affect their business. Knowing if your potential broker competes is certainly a question you'll want to ask. Competing brokers are not unlike other agents in that they are trying to sell and list properties to make commissions. While this doesn't necessarily present a chasm between you and the broker, it certainly is something worth considering.

The largest majority of top producers interviewed advised newer agents to avoid competing brokers, at least at first. This is not to insinuate that there is anything immoral or improper about a broker who wants to sell real estate. There are many well-respected, community-involved brokers who sell real estate. This is particularly true in offices with fewer agents-the commission splits are not adequate enough for the broker *not* to sell real estate. And, as a matter of course, there are many well-established agents who aren't swayed one way or the other when it comes to broker competition. Why then, is it different for newer agents?

Newer agents need support, training, and guidance. The broker who does not compete for listings or sales is able to offer this 100% of the time. Also, many of those who were interviewed made a logical assessment: The best brokers are managing the office all of the time, not worrying about their own listings and sales. Working for a broker who may have his own interests in mind, is better left to agents who are well established in the field. Additionally, non-competing brokers often have a referral program of some kind, offering their agents personal or professional referrals since they themselves do not perform standard sales activities.

A broker is not unlike a parent, a coach, or even an umpire; someone who is there to make sure the game is being played fairly and by the rules. This is not to imply that a competing broker cannot provide exceptional support and create a fun and motivational working environment. Just be aware of the implications associated with a competing broker and be sure to add inquires about this to your list of interview questions.

Training/Mentoring/Office Support

Training

We've already noted how important training and support are, as a matter of fact, they are important enough to deserve a section of their own. Training, mentoring, and, support are three different issues. The broker you are considering might be outstanding at providing one, but not so supportive on the others. While all three are important to consider and look for when selecting a broker or firm to work with, you may only feel strongly about one or two. Understanding all three of these is vitally important to your real estate career.

Training is probably the most important consideration of the three. Training can encompass a variety of factors, but an agent who is untrained, is like a loose cannon. It is easy to assess then, that training is a fairly important consideration for the broker as well. The difference is, that some brokers will provide extensive and ongoing training, while others will not.

Professional Profile

Mitzi Romiti, GRI

MitziRomiti@juno.com

Jobin Realty, Falls Church, Virginia

Years in Business: 17

"The first firm an agent goes to work for should offer training. Classes in all phases of real estate. Just having the licensing classes does not give the information REALTORS® will really need. Writing contracts, financing, negotiations, and any of the many subjects needed to be successful in real estate, should be provided by the firm."

Real estate involves many laws and contracts that are changing all the time. Make sure you find a broker who keeps current on these important issues and shares the news with his agents. Most brokers hold weekly office meetings to share this kind of critical information, others may leave their agents a lengthy voice mail to share important updates. At any rate, understanding the laws and practices as they relate to your industry is a crucial to your success. When you are busy listing and selling homes, it is not always possible to decipher the newest contract revisions.

Brokers who take the time and make a priority of keeping their agents up to speed with important issues are brokers to be treasured. In addition to industry related issues, technology is another consideration. Many brokers are recognizing the importance of technology in the real estate arena and are making extra efforts to push their agents to the next level. A significant number of firms offer electronic-based forms, in-house database management, and at the very least, let the agents know about local computer training courses.

Without a doubt, a new agent should consider the positive implications that training will have on a budding career, and it is probably one of the most important things to consider when choosing a broker.

Mentoring

Some offices offer new agents a mentoring program. While it might not always be a program that is officially set in place, what it really boils down to is this: the newer agent works for a limited period of time with a well-established agent in the office. Might this be a form of training? Yes, however, for the sake of clarity, a mentoring program is different in that it is generally another agent from the office doing the training, as opposed to the broker. Further, mentoring is usually more related to office policy, transaction procedure, and working with clients.

Mentors might also offer support and direction before listing appointments or property viewing. Others may actually join you on your listing and selling appointment for support or back up. Overall, mentors are established REALTORS® who are willing to show you the ropes until you get the hang of things. They may actually be part of a compensated program established by the broker or simply someone who doesn't mind helping you out. As a matter of fact, they need not be "official" mentors at all.

Often there will be someone you can ask direction or guidance from. As a general rule, REALTORS® are more than affable folk, who will be happy to offer their advice and experiences simply for the asking. It is always a good idea however, to find out from the broker, especially when there is no mentoring program established, which agents he recommends you "model."

Office Support

Office support services vary tremendously and the variance is usually associated with office or firm size. A larger office will probably have a receptionist, secretary, and perhaps an office manager. More and more firms are hiring escrow coordinators, technical experts, and marketing directors. How this all affects you, once again, depends upon your specific needs and preferences.

The majority of real estate offices have a receptionist or a secretary, or both. Although, many smaller offices have limited staff, which translates into agents doing much of their own administrative work. Some REALTORS® prefer handling their transactions in this manner and some do not. There is, however, one obvious benefit to having someone else answer the phone, and that concerns ad calls.

Recall that when you are assigned "Floor time," you will be privy to every outside ad call that comes in. That means that when Mr. and Mrs. Buyer are out driving around, see a house they like with your company's name on it, they'll call your office and you being the one "on floor," will intercept the call. This is what floor time is all about; the opportunity for agents to pick up potential clients. Obviously, the more sellable the properties and the larger the inventory of the particular firm you select, the more calls that might come your way. So what does this have to do with office support?

Those offices that do not offer receptionists, secretaries, or some kind of telephone assistance, are often offices that expect the floor person to answer all the calls that come in. Some of these calls will not be productive calls, and what may be frustrating is spending time putting calls for other agents into voice mail, while you risk your ad caller hanging up and calling someone else. The good news is that most firms have advanced beyond this elementary stage. However, it is important to note, with all due respect, that there are a fair number of successful, independent brokers, who often assume all the office responsibilities alone, or with one or two other REALTORS® sharing the load.

The positive side about larger firms is that they often include a handful of experienced and skilled office support. It might be that there is someone who handles all the administrative duties, provides technical support, or coordinates escrow accounts. When first starting out in the business, you might find this extra support helpful.

Professional Profile

Sharon Basham
SmBasham@bellsouth.net
RE/MAX Preferred, Monroe, Georgia
Years in Business: 12

"If you want to avoid the initial "Broker Hopping," don't accept a broker's offer unless you have already examined other offers first. Talk not only to the broker, but ask him if you can talk to some of his agents. Remember that most "traditional brokers" make offers with promises of training and assistance, but once you're hired you might find you're all on your own. Get specific, ask lots of questions."

Broker Interview Check List

Questions to Ask

_____

_____

_____

_____

_____

_____

_____

_____

_____

_____

_____

Broker Contact Information

Name   Telephone/Email   Notes about Interview or Firm

_____
_____
_____
_____
_____
_____
_____
_____
_____
_____
_____
_____
_____
_____
_____
_____
_____
_____
_____
_____
_____
_____

A BROKER'S POINT OF VIEW

So now that a pretty substantial group of established REALTORS® has agreed upon what kinds of qualities new agents should seek in a broker, what about how the broker feels? What do brokers expect from these REALTORS® they are interviewing? Successful brokers seem to realize the important "people factor" that goes into running a real estate business. We asked a group of diverse brokers to offer new REALTORS® some words of wisdom, ranging from broker philosophy to what they look for in agents, and to what their take is on what makes or breaks a REALTOR®.

Professional Profile

Mike Santini
MasterBoss@aol.com
Prudential Goldenkey, Piscataway, New Jersey
Years in Business: 25
Number of agents: 20

"My philosophy is to give the client more than they expect, that's what makes a REALTOR® successful."

Interview With A Broker

Clay Sigg
Csigg@lyonrealty.com
Lyon & Associates, Fair Oaks, California
Manages: 65 agents, Entire Firm: 500 agents

What's your personal philosophy for REALTOR® success?

"My philosophy for success in the business is that if you do the right thing for the people that you come into contact with, it will inevitably come back to you in the right way. The real estate brokerage industry is an extreme cause and effect business. Whatever you give out, you get back. Whatever level of commitment you make to yourself and to your clients, you will be repaid in kind. In the long term, integrity, fairness, honesty, empathy, keeping your promises, and respecting others DOES count in this industry."

What advice can you give new agents, just breaking into the business?

"My advice to REALTORS® just breaking into the business is that everything matters and nothing is impossible. With the right thoughts and the right actions, a new REALTOR® can accomplish just about anything in real estate. Beyond breaking into the industry, those habits have to be set for the entire career. The most important word that a new REALTOR® must remember is "MOTIVATION." The agent shouldn't spend a lot of time with any buyer or seller who isn't really motivated to help you get your job done. Otherwise, when you need them to help the most, they will fight you. If the buyer and seller are both motivated in a real estate transaction, their transaction will close unless the REALTOR® either gets in the way of the close or doesn't do his or her professional duty."

What's the secret to success?

"It's important to remember that approximately 80% of your success as a REALTOR® is predicated on how well and thoroughly you prospect."

There is no doubt that every broker you come across will have his or her own distinct style, personality, and office policies. There are, however, several factors that many brokers will agree as to what they consider important, if not required, when they hire new agents. Before we consider these though, let's hear what a handful of brokers say about their personal philosophy on running a real estate office.

On the issue of to compete or not compete, there seems to be two valid sides and the arguments are very similar as they were from the agents' perspective. On the first hand, and probably the most popular point of view for larger firms, is that the brokers do not compete with agents for listings and sales. Many brokers agree that they are better positioned to provide the support and practical advice that their agents often ask for if they are committed to non-competitive sales. As a Coldwell Banker broker from the mid-west said:

> **"If I was worrying about generating my own sales, I wouldn't be nearly as available to my team."**

There were many agents who concurred with this theory, although a fair amount of well-established agents were not at all opposed to competing brokers. On the other hand, there are many mid to small-sized firms strongly scattered throughout the country where brokers list and sell properties right along side their agents. A Century 21 REALTOR® from Kentucky said that by getting out in the trenches, just as her agents did, she felt as though she was of more value:

> **"When I'm out there selling and listing properties and trying to survive, just like they are, there's a common respect that transpires, because we really are on the same team."**

Once again, the matter of broker competition and overall philosophy of the broker and the firm must be a personal choice that is made with your professional goals clearly in mind. While many REALTORS® might enjoy the independence of being their own boss, in a manner of speaking, REALTORS® are also, by nature, very social creatures. This is why often times the office environment and team spirit is so important to a number of REALTORS®. Fortunately, most brokers recognize this need to bond and often encourage participation in planned office events, golf tournaments, or even attending trade shows and real estate conventions as a team.

Professional Profile

Teena Turner
Jevans@micron.net
Evans Realty, L.L.C., Emett, Idaho
Years in Business: 24
Number of agents: 11

"Our Company philosophy is that we emphasize integrity, customer service, team players, community activity, and positive attitudes. Management hires with these things in mind. If the person doesn't fit that profile, they are not hired. We have a company summer barbeque, an annual company business planning session, that includes individual agent business plans, and a company holiday party. Our agents are strongly encouraged to always participate in local town events and issues. We are actively involved in our city and county planning and zoning activities, chamber, local and state REALTOR® Associations."

Understand the broker's philosophy, his or her priorities, and the overall "feel" of the office. Talk to other agents, asking for their input about the office and the firm. When you're talking to agents in the office, ask yourself, "Is this someone I could work with, ask for advice from?" Even if you plan on working much of the time from your home office, finding a firm that you feel good about belonging to is critical to your long-term success.

How Important is the Broker Connection?

Regardless of what part of the country or what size the firm, most brokers agree that the relationship they hold with their agents must be one that is based on mutual respect, honesty, and ethics. You must feel that your broker is someone you can take your worst transaction to, admit it if you made a mistake, even a major one, and ask for professional guidance. Your broker will do everything he can to protect you, but honesty is essential. You cannot expect your broker to solve a problem for you if you haven't laid all your cards on the table. The broker who hires you sees you as an agent with potential-that doesn't mean the broker doesn't expect you to make mistakes-he does, however, expect you to come forth with those mistakes, not only for your own protection, but for the overall protection of the firm. If you don't feel that the connection with a broker could be a strong one, keep interviewing until you find one that fits.

Professional Profile
Judie McConville
JudieMc@ivnet.com
Prudential McConville Realty, Ottawa, Illinois
Years in Business: 26
Number of agents: 15

"The broker relationship is very important. I come from a comparatively small town with a population of 18,000. Our firm is one of the largest in town. I like the feeling of being on a team in my office. My agents have been with me for an average of 15 years. We are like a family here and know how one another thinks and reacts."

Professional Profile
Laureen Campbell
Laureenc21@aol.com
Century 21, New Milford, New Jersey
Years in Business: 24
Number of agents: 14

"The broker relationship is EXTREMELY important! A good producer needs constant encouragement, support, and advice- and they need a broker they can count on."

What Do Brokers Look For When Hiring REALTORS®?

Brokers have much more responsibility than merely hiring people to list and sell homes. Yes, the final goal is to close as many transactions as possible, but in this case, the broker has to be just as concerned with the journey as he is with reaching the final destination. A broker will ultimately be held responsible for all actions of his agents. Clearly then, a broker must demand the agents working under his license act within the highest code of ethics. This again, is why virtually all brokers insist that their agents participate in organized real estate. Honest and ethical behavior is probably the first criterion a broker will consider when hiring a new agent.

Professional Profile

Gene Goedker
goedker@goedker.com
Goedker Realty, Brainerd, MN
Century 21, New Milford, New Jersey
Years in Business: 35
Number of agents: 8

"The number one thing I look for in an agent is HONESTY- that's critical! Next important is their ability to stick with it for over a year and to be willing to spend their own time and money to self-promote."

Honesty, integrity, and team spirit run high on the requirement list for many a successful broker. Along these same lines, many brokers noted the importance of outstanding customer service, client follow up, and overall dedication to the real estate business. The other primary component most brokers seek is a fairly obvious one and pertains to the ambition and enthusiasm of the REALTOR®.

If a REALTOR® isn't willing to commit to the act of building a strong client base and moving inventory, than the broker probably won't be too interested in wasting the desk space. Every desk, computer, form, and support staff dollar is spent with the end goal in mind: to close multiple transactions. That being the case, brokers are not allowed the luxury of "carrying dead wood." That is not to say that brokers do not recognize the learning curve and the time it takes for new REALTORS® to build a client base. It is to say however, that eagerness to learn, cold call, do floor time, hold open houses, and general efforts to self-promote are expected, even from the greenest of agents.

> *Professional Profile*
> Becky Hill
> Hillbeck@kw.com
> Keller Williams Realty, Houston, Texas
> Years in Business: 20
> Number of agents: 90
>
> "What does a broker look for in an agent? Integrity, determination, self-motivation, and a desire to learn how to constantly take their career to new levels."

Some brokers noted that they prefer to hire experienced agents instead of new ones. While anyone can surely understand the reasons, such as not needing to worry about the initial no-production period, training costs, and, learning curves, many brokers, from virtually all firms, are willing to invest their time and company dollars into bringing up a new agent…when the agent shows potential.

> *Professional Profile*
> Betty Bezemer
> annw@kw.com
> Keller Williams Realty
> Years in Business: 21
> Number of agents: 43
>
> "Our company is dedicated to creating a motivating and empowering environment that helps our people achieve their highest sales productivity, leadership development, and life-achievement potential. The broker agent relationship in this firm is very strong. The associates trust me to lead them in the right direction legally, ethically, and help them to develop as true professionals."

In summary of what brokers say they're looking for, it seems to really boil down to two areas. The first commitment real estate professionals must make is to uphold the code of ethics. You must always be honest and forthright and remember that your broker is ultimately responsible for your actions. Again, this is where joining your local, state, and national associations can be of the greatest assistance. Still under the umbrella of ethical behavior lays the REALTOR'S® responsibility to operate with genuine concern for the client, which always includes outstanding follow up and customer service. The second necessity is the drive to succeed. This is not to say that you are required to be a high-energy super seller (although many top producers are), but instead it means that you must be committed to the profession, and as the old saying goes, actions speak louder than words. Enthusiasm and eagerness to learn are paramount to your success. Jump right in there and ask questions, take classes, study contracts, get busy promoting yourself to the public. If you've created an effective and challenging business plan, share it with your broker for feedback. Get busy!

What's Some Good Advice For New REALTORS®?

Brokers, like agents, have many mixed opinions on what it takes to become a top producer. The advice they offer is very similar though. From a broker's perspective, please recall, it's not only the agent's commission that is at stake, but the well being of the entire firm. So while brokers all have a vested interest in having their agents succeed, there are many other components a broker must contend with. A broker is not unlike a parent who needs to be fair and just with all his children. There will be agent rivalry, healthy competition, and occasional disagreements between agents wherein the broker will need to intercept. Among all of this, there will also be the need to keep what is in the best interest of the continued growth of the firm in mind. Periodically, this causes conflict and it would be an understatement to insinuate that the role of broker is anything less than remarkable. It is with this in mind that it is easy to understand the advice that many brokers offer new agents revolve around learning and motivation.

Professional Profile

Val Murphy
Ladera Realty, Inc., Los Angeles,
California   www.laderarealtyinc.com
Years in Business: 20
Number of agents: 15

"Any agent who expects to be successful in real estate must first and foremost adhere to ethics in the real estate industry. Also, whether an agent is full time or part time, effective time management is crucial. Consistency in marketing is another important success factor; if you make 10 cold calls per week, continue that schedule, real estate is a numbers game. Furthermore, a critical element for success is to exhibit professionalism at all times and treat ALL clients as though they are your most important. From the client purchasing a $70,000 condo to a $5,000,000 mansion, customer service is vital. Finally, always listen, listen, listen."

Learning

Because the role of broker is such a tremendous one, it would be ridiculous to think, especially starting out, that your broker will be the sole source of your training. Many brokers advocate that the best agents will spend some of their own time keeping current in their trade. Continuing education, reading publications, talking to top producers, and regularly attending both office meetings and MLS meetings are all excellent means for staying in the know.

While most brokers would agree that training is vital for new agent development, many brokers will concur that spending time with an established agent in the office is an exceptional way to learn the ropes.

Professional Profile

Terry Jacobs
Sherman@shermanco.com
Sherman & Company REALTORS®, Kerriville, Texas
Years in Business: 28
Number of agents: 15

"Get with someone who can offer some kind of a mentor program. I do not compete with my agents, I strictly manage- new agents need to talk to other agent who are out in the field beside them and who can mentor them along the way."

Remember, while it's wonderful to work like and model top producer behavior, it's not necessary that your mentor be a top producer. Clearly, there are hundreds of thousands of REALTORS® in this country who might not qualify at "top producer" status, and sometimes, this is by choice-as in the case of a second career, for example. At any rate, these well established REALTORS® can make exceptional mentors, particularly when it comes to understanding the market, understanding the process of completing transactions in your office, and general issues that a newer agent needs to be apprised of. In addition, those well-established steady producers may have more time to spend with someone who is still "green," and their input and experience is every bit as valuable as any advice you might read. Once you have gotten your feet wet and understand how the business operates as a whole, search out REALTORS® whose sales status you admire and move forward with more mentoring. Ask your broker to recommend one or two agents that might be willing to offer you some mentoring support.

Along the same lines of learning, falls the subject of technology. Brokers today want new agents who are either technology savvy or who are willing to get that way. Computer skills are not that difficult to acquire, and, while any new endeavor can first appear overwhelming, we will see in the technology chapter that incorporating technology into your real estate business is no more challenging then figuring out how to write your first offer.

Professional Profile
Don Plourde
dplourde@mint.net
DeWolfe Plourde Real Estate, Waterville, Maine
Years in Business: 17
Number of agents: 23

"We embrace technology and educate our agents as to the benefits technology can bring into their business…such as email marketing."

Motivation

Yes, we've already mentioned that brokers look for agents who are enthusiastic, but even beyond that as a prerequisite, many brokers suggest that motivation is paramount for any REALTOR'S® continued success. This is a business that can be feast or famine, when the market is good and inventory is high, interest rates low and buyers galore, it doesn't take a whole lot of motivation to keep going. During these crazy but gloriously busy times, a cell phone and a good organizer is about all the motivation you will need. However, this is also a business that will have some months when you feel sure you'll never sell another house. If you've saved wisely (as we'll discuss in the money chapter) you will probably be able to reduce your costs and squeak by. However, it's only with intense motivation that you can stay in the game. A substantial number of REALTORS® this year will no longer be actively selling real estate five years from now. While a solid client base and referral business will be the result of outstanding training, ethics, and customer service, none of those efforts will surface without motivation. Even when the market is less than perfect, your motivation must remain constant.

> ### Professional Profile
> Carmen Pappa
> Slwreal@aol.com
> St. Lucie West Realty, Port St. Lucie, Florida
> Years in Business: 25
> Number of agents: 22
>
> **"Never allow the word "no" to get in your way."**

By definition, motivation is simply the drive to proceed, to continue and to get the job done; the internal force that urges you onward, regardless of external factors that threaten to drag you down. We'll take a look at some great ideas for keeping yourself motivated in a later chapter, but for now, understand that motivation is an asset that all top producers must possess. The drive to succeed can be easily acquired, and that's good news, because it is an essential part of your career.

Sometimes, picking up the phone is the last thing you want to do. Luanna Vaughn, with Davis and Davis in California confided,

"We all have days when we wake up and think, I've got nothing in escrow, and even though that's when you want to stay in bed, that's when it's most critical you don't….you've got to keep yourself up and busy and in contact with clients."

What Makes it or Breaks it?

By the very nature of their businesses, brokers perhaps have the best vantage point of what makes an agent succeed or fail. While all of the aforementioned qualities are critical to sales success, and that's why brokers seek them out, the agents who succeed have some certain traits that are undeniable. In a word, commitment would probably best encompass the key to successful real estate sales. Commitment can be best demonstrated by someone who has made a conscious choice to dedicate his or her professional efforts to selling and listing homes.

Professional Profile

Donna Goings
Donnago@cville.net
Colonnade Realty, Charlottesville, Virginia
Years in Business: 15
Number of agents: 10

"You must be willing to make real estate a lifestyle, not just a job. You must be totally committed to learning and well versed in the technology needed to function in the business."

And of course, customer service is vital.

Professional Profile

Rick Stein
R@rstein.com
Re/Max Bayshore Properties, Traverse City, Michigan
Years in Business: 21
Number of agents: 21

"Consistency and customer follow up are crucial to success."

Customers, clients, and potential clients are truly the basis of your business. In addition to the homes you are selling, they are the single most important component to the industry. Without clients, you have no commission checks. It is therefore important to remember the vital role every person you meet might play; you never know if the next person you meet might be looking to list their home, act accordingly. Moreover, remember the human connection. Buying or selling a home is a pretty big deal to most consumers and therefore, customer relations are critical. As a matter of fact, the lack of customer care and good communication skills can be the doorway to your failure. This is such an important topic that you will find the next section dedicated to it.

Failure is not a subject that's necessarily fun to talk about, however, if you're committed to becoming a super-selling REALTOR®, you may as well be aware of the culprits that brought others down before you. As with any career in sales, assertiveness is important. Even, aggressiveness to some degree may be warranted, but the agent who is interested only in racking up the commission checks and not at all caught up in the joy of serving people, might as well find a new career.

This is a people business first, a property business second. If you can't get along with people, you can't sell real estate. As one Arizona agent put it, **"The people are the product, the house I sell them, the packaging."** So yes, the packaging is an important consideration, but remember, above all else, that it is your relationship with the client, that is the real deal.

> *Professional Profile*
> Bruce Curington
> BruceCurington@REALTOR.com
> Rossum & Neal REALTORS, Rapid City, South Dakota
> Years in Business: 9
> Number of agents: 20
>
> **"The biggest contributor to success for an agent is the desire and willingness to learn and try new things. The biggest failure? Unwillingness to learn and try new or uncomfortable things and failure to go the extra mile."**

In essence then, brokers look for agents who are honest, committed, and motivated. They care about the financial success and future potential of their agents and their firm. They recognize that customer service and follow up are vital and that a lack of customer concern can bring things toppling down in a hurry. We also looked at how important a broker's personal and professional philosophy may or may not be to you. You are now supplied with a list of considerations that brokers will be thinking about when they interview you for potential employment.

All in all, when you choose a broker and a firm, and a broker chooses you, you are engaging in a kind of marriage, and therefore, both parties should enter with care. Next we will begin the relevant journey into understanding the importance of proper communications with those we work most closely with.

COMMUNICATION SKILLS REALLY DO COUNT: PART II

"There is nothing so annoying as to have two people talking when you're busy interrupting."

Mark Twain (1835-1910)

Working With Clients

Effective communications skills is, without a doubt, the most important quality you will need to develop in order to be successful in real estate sales. Not only do the words you utter strongly influence the action of others, but your response to others' speech, as well as your own actions, are equally important in developing and maintaining effective communication skills.

While it's essential to understand Communication skills 101, it is also critical to know exactly whom you are communicating with. Buying or selling a house can be a very emotional experience for many of the clients you will work with. To that end, possessing a certain basic understanding of your clients' position, as well as some effective techniques for overcoming the more common objections, will set you on your way to improved communications and increased commission checks.

Communication Basics

Real estate transactions are often overflowing with emotion. First of all, both buyers and sellers are making gigantic financial and emotionally driven decisions. Second, REALTORS® tend to be high-energy people who are dependent on closed transactions to make a living. When you put clients who are highly emotionally charged, along side a couple of motivated REALTORS®, then add a problem to the mix...things can get explosive. People get mad; they sue, call your broker, cancel the listing or decide not to buy the house. The good news is that while effective communications can't resolve every professional issue that arises, it can certainly serve as a prelude to smoothing the waters whenever they get rough, as well as to help ensure continued business from clients who appreciate your efforts.

Professional Profile

Marilyn Doyle

Powellre@ncia.net

Peter W. Powell Real Estate, Lancaster, New Hampshire

Years in Business: 2

"Communication is my personal key to successful relationships. I have found myself back peddling on several occasions. Perhaps this is a result of not ascertaining immediate feedback regarding discussions or perhaps it is the involvement of numerous others giving their personal spin on discussions."

Listen, Listen, Listen

If you asked a half a million REALTORS® the most important communication skill they could think of, it would probably be listening. If the old "location, location, location" stands true as the three most important things about real estate, then "listen, listen, listen" are the three most important things about real estate sales. If you have an abundance of energy and can hardly wait for someone to finish talking so that you can respond to what it is they haven't even finished saying yet, then you might be a candidate for lessons in listening.

One method of ensuring you've been listening well is to play back what's been said to you. Not only does this show that you've paid close attention, but it also gives you a chance to absorb what has been said and prepare yourself with an intelligent response. Often times, this simple act can eliminate an abundance of future frustration.

Remember, that everyone's communication efforts are subject to their experiences, education, and a host of other factors that will clearly make communications easy for some, challenging for others. This is why in addition to simply making sure you understand the questions being asked or the statements being made, you should reiterate them for clarity. For example, if an ad caller is on the phone inquiring about a house he has just driven by and he asks you, "Is it nice inside?" How are you going to respond? Well, of course you'll offer an honest, yet positive answer, but is that enough? And, if you simply confirm that yes, the property is indeed nice inside, what have you learned about this prospect and what has he learned about you? If you're already a salesperson at heart, then you know all about the validity of open-ended questions.

The potential client question noted above could easily warrant a whole host of responses and questions, contingent on the property and the caller's tone. Let's try this scenario again:

"Is it nice inside?"

"Yes. It's lovely, how many bedrooms are you interested in?" Or,

"Well, it's an exceptional investment but it needs a little work. Who would be living in it?" Or,

"You bet it is, and wait until you see the master bath, when can I show it to you?" Or,

"It's very nice inside, in fact, the seller's have just painted and re-carpeted-when would you like to see it?

Obviously, there might be another hundred questions you could ask or things you could tell them about the property, but you get the idea. This is simply the act of responding positively with an open-ended question, and you'll need to become an expert in this area. Whether you practice on friends and family, read books, or talk into a tape recorder, learning to respond with open-ended questions will be one of the most important sales communication skills you will ever use. Also, let's talk a moment about the repeat-back theory.

Clearly, when emotions and adrenaline are running high, miscommunications come easy. Never will it be more crucial for you to exhibit your effective communications skills than at this particular time. We noted early the importance of repeating what you've heard. Not only does this serve to show the prospect that you've really listened to what he's saying and that it's worthy of your consideration, but it gives you an opportunity to truly absorb what's being said. Again, because our communication skills may be biased to our individual style, not clarifying can be a big mistake. Consider the following: You're showing a buyer a property and thinking you've done a good job in meeting his demands of a "Big" house.

"No," He tells you, this isn't what I want." You're confused, you've shown him a dozen homes, all meeting the criteria of "bigness," and you're convinced that this is a buyer who seems to be a little fickle. Finally, on a whim, you show him a property at the edge of town, small lot, average size square footage, and he falls in love with it, writing an offer on the spot, what happened?

Professional Profile

Joyce Whitfield

Joyce@joycewhitfield.com

Latter & Blum, Incorporated, New Orleans, Lousianna

Years in Business: 12

"I'm here to coach and clarify- the client has to make his own choice."

In many cases, simple clarification can make all the difference in the world. When a client is specifically asking for a particular quality or feature in a property, they must think it's important. However, just because his description means one thing to you, it might mean a completely different thing to him. In the above example, a lot of time could have been saved if we simply clarified the meaning of the word "big" as the client saw it. Here, the client had fond memories of the tiny house he grew up in, with the open-airy kitchen where his mother used to bake. Maybe he didn't realize exactly what he was looking for and maybe he couldn't discern that the feeling, an "open and airy" kitchen, was altogether different than "big." In his mind, an open floor plan meant big, and all the while, you were looking for footage. By playing back the communication and then clarifying it, you not only save yourself a lot of wasted time, but you also endear yourself to your client. In addition to saving time, this format is very effective in overcoming obstacles.

Professional Profile

Lydia Vannucchi

Lydia@lydiav.com

Prudential Tropical, Port Richey, Florida

Years in Business: 18

"Know yourself and what you're good at an grow from there. While other people talk about first time buyers, I call mine "last time buyers." This is a retirement community and purchasing that last home can be very emotional, but also very rewarding. I'm tied to the community and enjoy 100% referral business. Have a niche, know it well, and work hard to understand what your clients need from you."

Because, as we've already noted, this is a highly charged industry, you will undoubtedly come across buyers and sellers experiencing stress, confusions, and a menagerie of other emotions. Here is where effective communications will be put to the test and if properly used, your need to be a mind reader might be greatly reduced…but not completely. In the example of the buyer who was looking for something big, it was simply a matter of clarification; issue in understanding that would have been nipped in the bud with a little discussion. In some instances however, more skill and technique will be required.

There will be times when it is necessary to exercise your effective communication skills in a way that requires your most astute sense of awareness. And, it is at these times when listening to what's being said, might not be quite enough. It is at these times when listening to what's *not* being said is the answer. Every successful salesperson possesses at least a touch of mind-reading ability, intuition, or "gut feeling," and in this business, you might find that you need it.

When working with clients or prospective clients and finding yourself frustrated because you're addressing the needs that they've voiced, consider those that they haven't. Generally speaking, your clients aren't holding out on you, but rather, may not be actually aware of their specific needs and therefore have been unable to express them, leaving you in the challenging position of resolving these "mystery needs." Here is where communication expands beyond simple open-ended questions.

For example, a woman is selling her home because all of her children have moved out and she's tired of seeing all the empty rooms and wasted space. She really misses her children. She tells you though that she's looking for something small and you show her every house on the market; she likes nothing. After reading between the lines, *hearing more than what she's verbally given you*, you finally deduce that yes, she wants a smaller house, but the houses you've been showing her, would not allow enough space when her children come home from college to visit. What she wanted was a *different* house so that she wasn't reminded each day of the empty feelings she had inside. Size was really an irrelevant factor. Not only do you need to hear what's being said, but also it's equally important to hear what is not being said.

Professional Profile

Carolyn Egan

Carolyn.Egan@gte.net

Coldwell Banker Kattmann REALTORS®, Evansville, Indiana

Years in Business: 25

"Listen to them! Quite often they want something completely different than what they are saying or you are thinking. Remember that you are the professional and know more about the business than they do…. they're counting on you."

Your personal style, insight, and sales technique will eventually become your guiding light to assisting your clients and meeting their needs. From the example offered above however, you are hopefully beginning to see that selling houses is much more complex, challenging, and rewarding, than merely placing people and properties. Each case will present unique obstacles that will require you to apply your astute and growing ability to communicate effectively, read between the lines, and confer on the same level as your clients.

Listen, Listen, Listen.

One REALTOR® summed it up best with a reminder that we all have two ears and one mouth and should use them accordingly.

Professional Profile

Anna Paige Durant
Apdurant@sc.rr.com
Russel & Jeffcoat, Columbia, South Carolina
Years in Business: 15

"Be a listener first, don't be thinking of what you want to say and tune them out, or worse, act as though you know everything and they do not. Ask these folks for their opinions, ask their permission to do certain things- for example, "May I call the seller and find out for certain about this issue? Finally, don't try to solve all your client's problems. They need to take an active role or they will be fully dependent upon you. Keep the communication going so that client can figure things out…. they will love you for it!"

It is by no coincidence that people who listen well are considered more intelligent, kinder, and more enjoyable to be around. Listening helps to resolve issues, particularly when, often times the real quest is an avenue for the client to vent their frustrations—not a counter attack. As a sales associate, you'll want to learn not only to listen with all of your might, but also how to fend off those attacks that seem to be headed your way.

Keeping a cool head is probably right up at the top of the list when it comes to communicating wisely. As we've already stated, this can be an emotionally intense industry. While much of your experience in real estate sales will be overflowing with the joy of cashing many commission checks and making numerous clients happy homeowners and satisfied sellers, there are those days when escrow accounts come crashing down and you must be prepared.

You might receive a call from a seller who you just had a nice cup of coffee and conversation with an hour before. You pick up the phone and he is screaming something about the termite damage that he's not about to pay for. Here's a little lesson on developing thick skin.

It is inevitable, and not at all restricted to the real estate industry, that people will get upset. They will get mad, yell, and demand results. Again, listening is the number one key when these situations arise. Most of the time an angry client just needs to be heard and reassured that you're on his side. Many customer service focused books, not at all related to the real estate business, have indicated that the most important thing to remember when dealing with an angry client is to listen and empathize. This is where many of us make a mistake.

It is quite common to find yourself feeling defensive under attack-it's human nature. In this business however, it's fairly important that you put your personal feelings of needing to be right aside and work hard to serve your clients. Of course, this doesn't mean that you should ever feel compelled to subject yourself to profanity, disrespect, or abuse. It is to say however, that getting yourself worked up and shooting out your own ammunition in defense, will not solve anything, and it will certainly intensify the negativity of the situation. Here is where keeping the end goal in mind can truly save the day.

SEE THE END GOAL…ALWAYS!

By keeping your sights set on the end goal, from the start of each transaction, you keep yourself in the driver's seat. Staying in the driver's seat helps to keep you professional, courteous, and focused at all times, even in the face of adversity. Because the number one problem in any deal gone bad usually is a direct result of faulty communication, it would do you well to always remember and keep your communications calm and effective, and headed in the right direction.

Because the average real estate transaction will keep you in constant contact with your client for a minimum of thirty days (the low), up until sometimes a year (high), you're bound to see some ups and downs. It's important here to remember that even though *this* transaction is over in 65 days, the whole idea is to retain the client for the *next* transaction and certainly for on-going referrals. It's critical then, that you use this time as an opportunity to exhibit your outstanding communication skills. When things go wrong, your client might panic or become angry, he will expect you to find a solution, even if that solution is simply hearing what he has to say. Sometimes this will present quite a challenge and here is the question to ask yourself in order to avoid saying something you might regret.

Professional Profile

Roz Levine, CBR, CRS, GRI
Simakatz@aol.com
RS Residential, Wochester, MA
Years in Business: 15

"Work with clients and listen to their needs. Be patient and keep the big picture in mind. The commission check will come, but professionalism, communication, and service are the key ingredients."

Will this bring me closer to my goal?

There is an infinite number of examples, but one should suffice:

Situation: Your client is angry because his neighbor says you priced the house too low, he calls you and infers that you were looking for a "quick sale."

Your automatic Internal reaction: You're defensive, you feel as if you've been blind-sighted, attacked. Nothing could be further from the truth. You have two choices. The first choice:

1) Tell him he's crazy if he thinks the property could bring in a penny more. You did your homework and priced the property according to the market. You are indignant at his accusations.

Unfortunately, this response might be the first one you're tempted to spout out, but it is nonetheless, the wrong one. It is our human nature to respond defensively when we feel as if our credibility is in question, but it's not usually the most effective way to keep deals together. Consider what would happen if this was the response you offered your client. Chances are he would pull the listing and you would lose his current and future business. This wasn't a bad client, just one who was a little nervous and needing some reassurance, and, had you not gotten so defensive and retorted back in anger, you would have seen this. So here is the one question you need to ask yourself in virtually all communication efforts (and this is in no way limited to client communications!):

Will this bring me closer to my goal?

It's worth repeating a hundred times until you are certain you have gleaned the valuable insight that this simple question represents. While the primary goal in most every case will undoubtedly be holding the deal together and closing the escrow, there will be mini-goals along the way. Mini-goals are those immediate goals that pop up and have a direct affect on the success of the transaction. In the instance noted above, the end goal is to sell the client's property. The mini-goal, or the immediate goal, is to resolve the issue of his uneasiness about the listing price. If you apply the first choice, what do you imagine the result will be? Will it bring you closer to either of your goals? Probably not.

Keeping the end goal in mind, to sell his property, and the mini-goal, to calm him down, would both be more likely with this choice:

2) Ask him why he thinks the neighbor said that. Calmly remind him that you presented him documentation showing what the current selling prices were in the neighborhood. ***Read between the lines.*** He probably isn't mad at you at all. He's probably just afraid that he's committing some kind of financial suicide. Moreover, he's probably acting in direct defensive to what his neighbor said to him and he's expecting you to reassure him. Listen to what he has to say, repeat what he's said, calming him all the while.

Not only will choice two bring you much closer to your end goals, it will also be much more likely to bring you your ultimate and on-going goal of repeat and referral business. A REALTOR® with a calm demeanor, regardless of the circumstances, is one who people will feel confident entrusting their most prized possessions with. It wouldn't be true or fair to say that every transaction turns out perfect. It would certainly be accurate however, to state that virtually every transaction you encounter would serve as a learning-post for the next. While it might not seem like much of a consolation to discover when funding fell through, your buyer is distraught, the seller and his agent hate you, that you are eventually going to prosper from this advice; but you will. Remind yourself daily:

Always keep a cool head.

Keeping your end goals in mind is truly the secret. That doesn't mean of course, that you're not subject and expected to release your frustrations in private. Scream and shout when you can, but never to or at anyone else you are working with, not the client, not the other agent, not the escrow officer, and not the lender. It doesn't do any good and it marks you as unprofessional. Most importantly, it takes you farther away from your goals. It is essential that you establish yourself as someone who can stay sane and calm in the face of adversity...your clients are banking on it.

Professional Profile

Becky M. Popma
Bpopma@emeraldcoast.com
Coldwell Banker JME Realty, Niceville, Florida
Years in Business: 10

"Listen to your clients- acknowledge their situation. Keep calm and professional and give your advice. Remember: you are not making the decision, you are managing the sale."

Another helpful client communication tips revolves around understanding human nature.

Professional Profile

Sue Causey
Scausey@alynk.com
Coldwell Banker, Racine, Wisconsin
Years in Business: 14

"You should know something about personality traits, why people exhibit certain behaviors. Also, be aware of your own personality traits and how they interact with clients and others."

There are many wonderful books and audiotape programs that offer virtually any kind of communication and psychology-centered focus you might imagine. But, since many REALTORS® are "people-persons" anyway, they tend to have a fairly clear concept on how to deal with different personality types. It would be a mistake though to think that all clients are identical in needs, wants, or level of tolerance.

Clients are people and people come in all different shapes and sizes, personality types, and with challenges that will need to be dealt with accordingly. You will get the most benefits out of this diversity if you see each client and each challenge as a new opportunity to learn. Every transaction is like a lesson toward your overall education in the real estate industry. There is no single book or seminar that can provide you with a pat answer on how you will interact with your clients in every single circumstance; that would be impossible. There are, however, guidelines, as delineated here, that can be adapted and applied in a variety of situations. The most important thing, other than remembering to listen and to always act with integrity, is to incorporate your own personal communication and selling style in a manner that is consistent with what you feel the client *needs*.

Professional Profile

Trudy Ault
Trudyault@REALTOR.com
Rhoades Realty, Incorporated
Years in Business: 9

"Focus on concepts and let your clients speak as long as they want to. Make eye contact, take notes, and clarify any misunderstanding through open-ended questions."

Understanding that each transaction and each client you encounter will be somewhat different than the one before is the first step. There is no exact science or method when it comes to working with people. As a REALTOR® though, you will want to make every effort to ensure that the customer service you have provided your client with is nothing less than impeccable.

Professional Profile

Tamara Ross
Tross1214@aol.com
RE/MAX First
Years in Business: 15

"In working with clients, it is important to establish your boundaries and then gently but firmly not allow the lines to be crossed. There are times when it might be good business to refer a difficult client to another agent who might be able to work with them more easily. We're all just people, but if you don't get along with someone, move on."

It is not within the scope of this book to provide you with specific instruction on overcoming objections and challenges. If ever you find yourself in an uncomfortable or seemingly volatile situation, it is essential that you confer with your broker or other appropriate party. But, while working with clients is an ever-evolving and highly complex subject matter, there does seem to be some consistent challenges many REALTORS® find when working with sellers and buyers and they are ones you should become familiar with.

Working With Sellers

Sellers are the foundation of your business. They are the ones who provide the inventory that keeps the economy moving and the escrow accounts opening and closing. There are certain objections that tend to arise with sellers and it is important to understand them and approach them accordingly. Again, each circumstance will vary and each client will be unique, but by understanding some of the more frequent objections, you will be better equipped to develop your own response tactics.

Some of the most common occurrences that can cause conflict with sellers are listing price, commission costs, and sometimes even open houses. It must be understood at the start that selling a home often involves financial and emotional investments that cannot be taken too lightly.

Many REALTORS® recognize that sellers sometimes find it difficult to price their property objectively. They have a vested interest in their homes that often times bypasses logic and common sense when it comes to determining a listing price. Here is the perfect opportunity to recall your end-goal and read between the lines.

It is not unusual, depending on the circumstance, when you go to list a property, you are selling much more than just a house. Often times you are selling your client's memories as well. It may look like a tract home that needs a coat of interior paint, but perhaps it is the room where their child took a first step, or family holidays still echo through the halls. There might be a time when you are working with a client who is selling a recently deceased family member's home and finds it difficult, if not cold-hearted, to be business-minded. The point here is that there are often many emotions related to selling a home. As a REALTOR®, you need to be sensitive and responsive to your client's needs. Telling someone who is listing because they are getting a divorce that they picked a great time to sell, might not always be the most appropriate thing to say. Furthermore, don't be convinced that if you're working with a seller who's primary attachment to the property is one of investment, there will be no emotional impact…money is always subject to emotion.

Professional Profile

Phillip Lande
Plande@atlasrealty.com
RE/MAX Preferred, Fishers, Indiana
Years in Business: 20

"Be creative, play to the market, don't be greedy, share the listing information immediately, and above all, PRICE THE PROPERTY CORRECTLY THE FIRST TIME!"

Today, it is not unusual for REALTORS® to experience "listing interviews." A listing interview happens when a seller asks to meet with you to discuss listing a property but they inform you that they will also be meeting with other agents. Some sellers interview several agents before listing their property. Real estate sales is a highly competitive field, nevertheless, you must always remember to operate under the code of ethics that you are obligated to.

Professional Profile

James O'Connell, ABR,CIPS,CRP,CRS,GRI,E-Pro
Oconnell@Oconnellrelo.com
RE/MAX Partners, Fort Lauderdale, Florida
Years in Business: 21

"Be firm, but always, always, be honest."

It is important to understand that regardless of how many agents a prospective seller is considering, the offerings are all very similar on paper: an entry in the MLS system, a for sale sign in the yard, a lockbox, advertisements in the local newspaper, and open houses. It is easy to understand that if most agents are offering the same service with the same perks, a cut in commission might sway the sellers to sign on the dotted line, however, most REALTORS® rule against this, as we'll discuss. The main factor to a successful listing appointment and future sale is proper pricing.

Pricing a Property

Comparable Market Analysis (CMA), or comparisons, affectionately known in the industry as "comps," are critical to accurately pricing a property. A comp is a sold listing in the same vicinity as the potential listing. There are certain considerations made when working with comps such as square footage, property condition, improvements, and lot size. These factors should be considered in establishing a reasonable listing price. Different REALTORS® have different methods and it would serve you well to ask other agents in your office to offer their advice on a particular listing, prior to the appointment.

Professional Profile

Christel Silver
Christel@silverhouses.com
Realty Executives Ones, Gaithersburg
Years in Business: 18
"Be truthful and honest and refuse to overprice your listings."

Comparisons are important not only because they gauge the current market, but also because they serve as an excellent means for REALTORS® to price properties. It can clearly be a problem then when a property is overpriced and someone down the street demands to list at the same price. An example of this would be a neighborhood of houses where the average sales prices has been $125,000. That includes a little more for the home that features a built in swimming pool and a few other improvements, and a little less for the home that needs a new roof and landscaping. To come along and list a home well below this average or well above it, without considering the comparatively priced properties, is doing an enormous injustice to your seller.

It becomes obvious however, when an agent does fail to price accordingly, how that action can upset the applecart. Your sellers assure you that their property is in much better condition than the neighbor's is, and the neighbor's is listed at $140,000. Shouldn't theirs be listed at $145,000? It may be easy for you to immediately identify that the neighbor's agent has priced the property right out of the market, however, trying to explain this to your seller requires documented proof of an actual recorded sale. For example, often the best ammunition for this scenario might be to pull up from MLS the properties that have most recently *sold* in the neighborhood. This provides good solid evidence of what the current market will bare. Show this to your client, assuring him that the neighbor's property is indeed overpriced, as evidenced by the fact that it hasn't sold, and then let the seller make an intelligent choice that is based on all the facts.

You owe it to yourself, your industry, and above all, your clients, to not be temped to list a property higher than it is worth simply as a means of gaining the listing. Price it right the first time.

Professional Profile

Mark Jeffers

Mjeffers99@aol.com

Coldwell Banker The Broker's Realty Group, Warren, Ohio

Years in Business: 11

"In this business, no two transactions will ever be the same- be prepared for a different challenge every time."

Commissions

Commission costs can be another area of objection when working with sellers. Dozens of established REALTORS® have developed their own unique responses to overcome this obstacle. However, most REALTORS® will not cut their commissions, and rightly so. Selling a home requires skill, effort, and hard work, and the REALTOR® who sells it should be compensated accordingly. This is not to say that many a REALTOR® hasn't cut her commission before in order to make a transaction close…it happens. However, to say that unless special circumstances prevail, most REALTORS® acknowledge their worth and refuse to be undersold simply in order to acquire a listing.

The listing should be earned on merit and your ability to convince the sellers that you are the most qualified, enthusiastic, and determined person for the job. Also, remember to advocate that you participate in organized real estate and that by doing so, you are at the top of your industry and it is mandatory that you operate under a strict code of ethics.

All things being equal, it will be your personal style, your ability to communicate effectively and your success at convincing the sellers you will work harder than anyone to move the property. Then, stick to your promises. Be prepared with your knowledge about the area, and above all else…bring your comps! Now let's talk more about commission objectives.

Professional Profile

Sharon Basham
Smbashman@bellsouth.net
RE/MAX Preferred, Monroe, Georgia
Years in Business: 12

"Whenever you decide to cut your commission for someone, for any reason, count on that transaction being the most time-consuming and most difficult you will ever have."

Since commissions are what you to count on for survival, you may find yourself feeling a bit on the defensive side when a prospective seller challenges your worth. Here again is the perfect opportunity to apply the primary lesson of communications; listen, repeat back, and always, always, keep the end goal in mind. The situation might go something like this:

Seller: "Six percent? Jeez, that's nearly eight thousand dollars! You want me to pay eight thousand dollars to sell my house?"

This presents a valid concern, it is not at all unusual for the most reasonable sellers to feel overwhelmed when he actually considers the dollar amount and envisions a healthy chunk of his equity flying out the window. It's important that you remain calm in your response. Saying something like, "Well, you have no idea how difficult and time consuming selling this piece of property is going to be for me," probably wouldn't be a very effective response.

If you read between the lines then you've already noted that the seller is simply surprised and apprehensive about such a seemingly large dollar amount. Furthermore, if you are keeping the end-goal in mind, which at this particular point is to acquire the listing, then you'll recognize immediately that responding defensively is not going to bring you one inch closer to that goal.

An appropriate response might involve explaining why the percentage is an industry standard in your state or area. And, that it all really boils down to the tasks involved in selling a property. Assure the seller that you will work extremely hard to get him the highest dollar amount and the best terms possible. Calmly inform him that there are many things going on behind the scene, such as advertising, marketing, and negotiations. And finally, remind him that the cost of not using a qualified REALTOR® such as yourself, could undoubtedly end up costing him more. When sellers choose not to use a qualified REALTOR®, they could quite likely incur unwanted expenses (that might included lawsuits) that exceed the standard cost of commission. This is also a good time to reiterate that, when it's his turn to purchase, he won't be out a penny for your services, as commissions are almost always a seller responsibility. Often times that fact alone can make a seller, who is also going to be a buyer, feel better.

Virtually all REALTORS® have contended to some degree with seller objections to commission costs. It would behoove any new agent to talk with established REALTORS® to gain deeper insight and understanding as to the various practices established within your own firm. But most importantly, remember that this presents the perfect opportunity for you to demonstrate your effective communications skills, while always keeping the end goal in mind. Let's look at another area of interest.

Open houses, as stated earlier, are an effective means for meeting prospective clients; this applies to both new and established agents alike. Holding a house open will often inspire curious neighbors to stroll in, giving you the opportunity to meet them and establish yourself as an area expert.

Professional Profile

Luanna Vaughn
Luannav@pacbell.net
Davis & Davis & Associates, Carmichael, California
Years in Business: 15

"Open houses are great for meeting buyers and making your seller happy. They seldom sell listings. I'm usually working with buyers on the weekends, so I only hold a listing open if the seller really insists upon it."

Each meaningful connection you make in this business, could ultimately lead to a deal. Some agents feel that holding open houses is a waste
of time and would rather be working with their long list of buyers, while
other agents find value in the practice and consider it an integral part of
the listing agreement. This will vary from firm to firm and agent to agent.
At any rate, it is important to recognize that when you are attempting to
become established in the industry, especially in a particular area, open
houses rank right up at the top of the list for meeting prospective buyers
and sellers. Use this opportunity to your advantage.

When planning an open-house, some of the more common approaches
include advertising in the weekend paper, giving the address and hours the
property will be open, and placing signs on corners with arrows for people
driving by. General open house tips include turning lights on and opening
drapes, giving a bright and airy atmosphere inside. A guest book, a pile of
business cards, perhaps property brochures, are all important tools when
holding an open house. You'll want to follow up with any good prospects
who come to see the property and you'll want to report back to your seller
any feedback and interest that resulted from the open house.

Sellers then, provide one half of the transaction equation. With time,
effort, and careful communication skills, you will learn to overcome most
seller-objections. Remembering to listen, play back what's been said and
clarify the meaning, read between the lines, and above all else, always keep
your end goals in mind. The seller provides the product to be sold, now
let's consider the one that wants to buy it.

Buyers

Not unlike sellers, buyers are a critical part of the successfully-closed
real estate transaction. All of the inventory in the world would be worth-
less if there wasn't someone to buy it. Someone who is ready, willing,
and qualified!

Working with buyers can be an exhausting and exhilarating experience. Recognizing the buyer as someone who is probably making the biggest investment, both emotional and financial, of his lifetime, is crucial. So much so, that first time buyers deserve a section all of their own.

Buyers, particularly first time buyers, can be more time-intensive than sellers, generally speaking. Some agents have designated themselves as strictly buyers' or sellers' agents in order to concentrate on one side of the transaction, although this is not the norm; many REALTORS® may prefer or work primarily at one end of the transaction. This is not to say that they would turn down a listing or a buyer if one presented itself. While buyers can be rewarding to work with, they too can present challenges.

Potential communication conflicts with buyers usually center around financing, wasted weekends (showing properties), and buyer's remorse. First time buyers are full of good intentions and their enthusiasm can be contagious, however, there are some considerations to keep in mind when you're working with buyers. The joy of assisting in a first time home purchase is wonderful, and presumably, these first time buyers will be moving up in the world in 3-5 years and will call upon you to list and sell them a new home (assuming you've done a good job and maintained consistent follow up).

Professional Profile

Mary A. Kuhlmann, CRS
Mkuhlmanncrs@alltel.net
Woods Brothers, Incorporated, Lincoln, Nebraska
Years in Business: 11

"Transactions dealing with first time buyers seem to be the most rewarding, but they can be the most stressful too. The stress comes from the lack of funds on both sides, buyers and sellers, to deal with repairs that are required or needed."

Financing

While first time buyers may present more financial challenges, literally every buyer you work with should be pre-qualified. The following chapter will provide you with valuable insight into the world of lending, but for right now, simply acknowledge that pre-qualifying or pre-approving buyers is a necessity. Nothing is worse than spending a great deal of time with an enthusiastic buyer and finally writing an offer, only to discover the dream home will remain a dream because he cannot qualify for a loan.

This doesn't mean you can never show a property to prospective buyers without asking them to first meet with a lender. A good case in point, or two, would be ad calls and open houses. If someone drives by one of your listings and wants you to meet them so that they can see the inside, or likewise, if someone enters your open house and wants to explore, you're not going to turn them away. However, most REALTORS® would agree that either of these situations warrants the question, "Have you been pre-approved"

Professional Profile

Don King, ABR, CRS, GRI, SRES
Don@DonKingHomes.com
RE/MAX of Rancho Bernardo, San Diego, California
Years in Business: 11

"Never put a buyer in your car who is not pre-qualified or pre-approved for a loan and who has not committed, preferably in writing, to work exclusively with you."

Even the buyer who assures you that he has 25k socked away for a down payment may have forgotten about that previous bankruptcy or otherwise marred credit situation that prevents him securing a loan. Pre-qualifying your buyers will save both you and the buyer a significant amount of time, energy, and effort.

Another subjective challenge in working with buyers involves time spent showing property. Many well-established REALTORS® have a maximum number of houses, or weekends, they are willing to devote to a non-buying buyer. It would be impossible to say how many is too many and finding the perfect house can often be a challenge. It's a big invest-ment and buyers have the right to be picky.

Pre-qualifying your buyer may be the number one priority, but deter-mining your buyer's motivation is a strong second. Just because someone has been qualified to buy a house, does not necessarily mean they are motivated to move forward. Identifying the level of motivation in your buyer will give you a fairly accurate gauge as to how serious they are about writing an offer.

For example, if the buyer has a home that she has recently sold and only thirty days to vacate before escrow closes, you've got a motivated buyer on your hands. There are as many motivating factors as there are buyers and your job is to recognize and work with them. If your prospective buyer doesn't seem very motivated to buy, yet wants to "house-hunt" each and every weekend, you will need to call upon your own insight and the advice of those you trust to decide how you will proceed.

Working with buyers is every bit as critical as working with sellers when it comes to effective sales communication techniques. And, one of the initial areas you'll have to practice these techniques revolves around showing prop-erties. Any REALTOR® will agree that taking off half-cocked, flying from one property to the next, without first defining exactly what your buyer is looking for is sure to drive you crazy-and it will only confuse your buyer!

Regardless of how you acquire your prospective buyer, and after you have taken appropriate measures to pre-qualify them for a loan, you'll want to sit down and discuss exactly what the buyer is looking for. If this is a first time purchase, the buyer may not be sure. This is when you'll need to exhibit extreme patience and assume the role of counselor. Often times, first time buyers are completely ignorant of the many facets associated with purchasing property and will count on you to educate them. The process of contracts, loan applications, title, escrow, repairs, etc., is overwhelming in and of itself and then add to that the fear of making such a giant commitment... how can they even begin to think clearly about what kind of floor plan they need?

Professional Profile

Lisa Mathena

Lmathena@aol.com

Patterson Schwartz, Lewes, Delaware

Years in Business: 10

"Listen more than you talk, but when you do talk, be firm, intelligent, and honest."

While you will have to depend on your astute people skills to help you assess the best way to learn what kind of property will best suit your buyer, asking him is the first step. When you're working with couples, you'll often find that they have different desires. One partner, for example, may be primarily concerned with a large backyard for the children to play in and the other is more concerned with ample closet space. Make clear at the beginning that compromises will need to be made in some areas and then create a list of needs in order of priority.

It is no coincidence that often times buyers end up writing offers for properties that don't even come close to meeting their list of criteria. They told you they wanted two bathrooms, no matter what, and a two-car garage. Then, on a whim, they fall in love with a little one bathroom, single-car garage property that you weren't even going to show them, but your instinct made you do it. The truth is, that people fall in love with properties the same way they fall in love with other people-often without rhyme or reason. And the point you can gain from this is that while it's always effective to find out in advance what features your buyers are looking for, it's equally important to understand that they'll probably be willing to make allowances. Your buyers will know when they find a home that suits their fancy-your job is to help them.

Say you find the perfect home that fits your buyer's needs and they turn it down. What if you show your buyer ten properties that meet with his specific criteria and he still says no? If this is a buyer who, for example, has explicitly stated that he's looking for a three bedroom, two bath, two story house with a big enough garage for a work shop, and you've shown him a number of properties that meet each of those requirements, maybe there's a problem.

The problem could be that the properties you've shown him simply don't appeal to his tastes, or that he's really looking for some other feature that he just hasn't been able to identify. As his REALTOR®, you'll want to carefully consider whether or not there is anything you can do to help him recognize the issue so that you can take steps to search for the perfect property (or as close as you can get!).

Professional Profile

Bill Ayotter
Bill@spectrarealestate.com
Spectra Real Estate and Development, Traverse City, Michigan
Years in Business: 12

"Never take "NO" personally, just do your best and know your limits."

Sometimes however, the buyer is just not motivated to buy. This is where you will have to use your own good judgment in determining how you will proceed. If you feel confident, or at least hopeful, that you will find the house for your prospective buyer and that, as a result, you'll get the sale, plus the listing on his current home (that he mentioned he'd need to sell in order to buy a new one), then by all means, move forward. If you have nothing better to do but drive around each weekend showing him property, spending your valuable time and gas dollars on someone you are relatively sure is not going to be writing any offer anytime soon though, you'll have to ask yourself if you're heading in the right direction.

"There are always reasons not to make decisions, and some people don't want to make a decision, but if you don't make it on a timely basis, you miss the opportunity to move forward."

This is one of NAR President Richard Mendenhall's favorite quotes that he heard early on in his career, and has always kept in mind.

While dropping a buyer is a purely personal choice, many REALTORS® have acknowledged they may periodically need to do so. If you feel a buyer is not going to buy and you are confident that you have shown him every listing under the sun that even remotely meets his demands and you do decide to let him go, there are some things to keep in mind.

First of all, remember your effective communication skills. If it doesn't appear that you'll be writing any offers for this person, create an end-goal that says the time and effort you have put forth will reap you a future sale, listing, or perhaps at least a referral. In other words, why throw away all of the energy you just invested in this no-go buyer? If you simply drop him, you are burning a bridge that may one day lead to a potential transaction. Therefore, it is always best to approach the act of letting a buyer go in as gentle a manner as possible. Perhaps volunteer to call him once every few weeks and tell him the property addresses of new listing so that he can drive by them, on his own time, and check them out. If he responds with a request to see the inside, and you feel confident the roller coaster ride will begin again, kindly remind him that he's already mentioned he needs to sell his own house first, so if he's ready to list it, then you're ready to start showing properties again. Be firm, but kind. Stand your ground and sell it if you can!

Professional Profile

Chuck Glazer

Chuckglazer@REALTOR.com

Realty Executives, Fort Myers Florida

Years in Business: 35

"Do not waste too much time with lookers when you could be writing offers."

Professional Profile

Robert W. Southwick

Rswdl@aol.com

R.A. Weidel REALTORS, Princeton, New Jersey

Years in Business: 10

"You have to determine if they're motivated, and if they are, lead them in the right direction. If they are simply shopping and not buying, tactfully refer them to another agent."

Buyer's remorse is also known as "cold feet" and it is not unlike the cold feet some people experience before their wedding day. When a person is about to make a seemingly life-long commitment, both of their time and of their money, it is not at all unusual for them to feel fearful. As a REALTOR®, you will need to understand this fear and soothe it accordingly. Generally speaking, buyer's remorse centers upon the buyer making what they consider an enormous financial commitment. It commonly surfaces at the first sign of trouble or as a result of some external influence.

It is not at all unusual that the home inspection reveals termite or dry rot damage, for example, yet for a frightened buyer, this might be all he needs to step back from the entire transaction. It may be something big or something small, but it's something that scares him more than he already is and might indeed be just the thing that causes him to change his mind. Another fear factor centers upon outside influences.

A quite common scenario involves the buyer calling the REALTOR® and saying, "My mother thinks I'm paying too much for it…I'm not sure if this is such a good idea." Here, your typical and justified response might be the pit in your tummy as you see your commission check dissolving before your very eyes. You might feel angry and want to remind the buyer that this isn't his mother's house, but of course, this isn't any kind of response you would ever even consider giving. This is once again the perfect opportunity for you to come forth with your effective counseling and communication skills.

First of all, read between the lines. The buyer is feeling remorse and fear and someone has ignited the fire. Many REALTORS® have stories to share about a well-meaning mother-in-law or a not-so-well-meaning neighbor who made some kind of comment that instilled mounting fear in the buyer. It is not unusual for buyers to share their purchase experiences with their friends and co-workers, who, in retrospect, have bought or sold their own homes, making them house-selling experts (in their own minds). This is something you'll often have to contend with when working with buyers, so it's best to accept it early on and develop effective strategies for overcoming it.

Secondly, let's look at your goals. You're end goal, obviously, is to close the transaction. What about your mini-goal, the one that is immediate? Your mini-goal is to calm your buyer down and resolve the issue of the moment. Certainly, correcting him about his mother's appraisal skills would not be conducive to either. This is the time when you provide your professional support and reassurance, perhaps reminding him that he is perfectly qualified for the property and that it is the same price he is currently paying for rent but a much wiser investment (if this is the case, of course). Also, remind him of what he finds appealing about the property. If you've been a good, attentive listener, you will know what kind of buyer personality type you are dealing with and respond accordingly. If he's family oriented, assure him that he'll enjoy raising his children in that big back yard, or maybe it was the workshop in the garage, or the proximity to downtown. Whatever it was that made that the property worthy of writing an offer on, is the same thing you'll want to keep close at hand for moments like these.

Your job as a REALTOR® is to provide the most honest, ethical counseling you are capable of giving. Using the term "counseling" is very accurate in the business of real estate sales. Much of the time, buyer's remorse can be smoothed out with some solid re-evaluation between you and your buyer. Simply reassuring your buyer as to the positive points and benefits involved with continuing the transaction will be helpful. If, for whatever reason, the buyer chooses not to proceed with the deal, then the property probably wasn't right to begin with. It is critical that you develop effective communication skills and demonstrate a client-first way of thinking. Your people skills will be your strong suit and the single strongest determining factor for your ultimate and on-going success.

It's a people business first, a property business second

Just as in working with sellers, working with buyers should involve your utmost attention to ethics, ensuring that they are making a wise property investment, based on the information and knowledge you have made available to them. When dealing with first-time buyers, remember to be patient and supportive and realize that this is the kind of client likely to produce the most outside influence from friends and family members. When showing property, don't burn bridges. Future sales or referrals just might develop. It is also intelligent to know your limits as to when you've shown a single client too many properties, and it's time to move on. This all requires your careful consideration towards each client. Remember to read between the lines; gauge motivation, calm buyer's remorse, and respond effectively to whatever obstacles might pop up. Genuine concern

for your clients is without a doubt the single most important consideration for repeat and referral business.

Closing Gifts

Professional Profile

Luanna Vaughn
Luannav@pacbell.net
Davis & Davis & Associates, Carmichael, California
Years in Business: 15

"In most instances keys are delivered to buyers on the day of recording. I
find that this is usually a good time to present them with a
"congratulations" gift. It depends upon the buyers, but generally speaking,
a plant, a bottle of wine, or even a gift certificate is a nice touch."

Many REALTORS® show their client-appreciation in the way of closing gifts. A closing gift is simply a present to show your buyer or seller how
much you appreciate their business and to congratulate them on the purchase (or sale) of a new home. There is an added motivation to consider
when determining what kind of closing gift you'll want to purchase. Gifts
are a token of appreciation and a thank you for the business.

Professional Profile

Mickey Bradley
Sellsre@gate.net
RE/MAX 100 Riverside, Port St. Lucie, Florida
Years in Business: 17

"Community involvement and customer follow up is not only a
personal way to give back to those we work for and with, but it also
brings us back more repeat and referral business than anything we
do."

A closing gift is like a seal of completion that reminds the client what an effective REALTOR® you really are. When that client goes to sell his home, and/or, to purchase another, chances are he'll call you, the REALTOR® who treated him so well the first time around. In addition, remember all of the benefits of referrals this successfully closed client might provide you with. Chances are good that if your customer attentiveness, quick response time, and smart negotiating skills are topped off with a lovely "parting gift," you will reign high in the mind of the client, making you first on his mind when his cousin from Chicago is transferring to town, or any such opportunity that might lead you to future sales.

So how much to spend on the closing gift? First of all, there is no correct answer. Even among REALTORS®, regardless of geographic location. Some gauge it on the transaction amount, others on the likelihood of repeat or referral business, but most agree, a closing gift is essential. Closing gifts are tax write offs, at least up to a certain dollar amount, so you'll want to check with your accountant and keep your receipts. While $25 may be a standard rule of thumb, some REALTORS® who felt the transaction amount or chances of repeat business were good, acknowledge spending much more on closing gifts, considering them a wise investment.

If you've spent any amount of time with your clients, you should have a fairly good idea of what kinds of things might be appropriate for the closing gift. House ware products are always appropriate, as are plants, doorknockers, birdhouses, food, and flowers. A marketing tip is warranted here. While flowers and wine are lovely thoughts, consider the long lasting impact your present makes if it's something they see, or better yet, get complimented on, on a regular basis. What better reminder of what a wonderful REALTOR® you are then to think about you each time someone notes the lovely sounding chimes hanging from the patio?

Referrals and Repeat Business

While we're discussing the importance of client relationships and communications, let's take a look at the foundation of any top producer's business: referral and repeat business. One of the most lucrative components of this business is how your hard work and effort can have a real snowball effect. Once you have begun to establish yourself, however slightly, you will be amazed at how many clients can result from one good transaction.

If you sell one couple a home and they are happy with your efforts, they will then tell someone they might know who is looking for a house, all about you. They might also mention your name to someone who they know is selling. From one, or both of those leads, a new transaction is born. Then, the newer clients happen to know someone looking for a home, and one deal leads to another.

> *Professional Profile*
>
> Mickey Bradley
>
> Sellsre@gate.net
>
> RE/MAX 100 Riverside, Port St. Lucie, Florida
>
> Years in Business: 17
>
> **"Community involvement and customer follow up is not only a personal way to give back to those we work for and with, but it also brings us back more repeat and referral business than anything we do."**

Ultimately then, when you are selling a home for someone, you are also proving yourself to every person that your seller knows, is related to, works with, or might meet in the future. The same applies to buyers; you are showing property or negotiating terms for the buyer and everyone the buyer knows. The smartest REALTORS® recognize and survive on this very concept. It would be a grave injustice to move from one transaction to the next without keeping this concept well in mind. In addition, repeat business operates on a similar scale.

You've closed the escrow and the clients call you to list a rental property you might not have even known they had. And, of course, many buyers stay put for only a few years and then decide to "buy up;" invest in a bigger home. This will present an opportunity for you to not only sell them a new, more expensive home, but also for you to list the one you sold them to begin with. The possibilities are endless.

Successfully closed, well-worked transactions will linger in the minds of your clients for a long time. Obviously, the opposite is also true.

By exhibiting outstanding customer service and working hard to negotiate the best deal possible for your clients, you will always be viewed in a positive light for referrals and repeat business. Of course, it's up to you to let your clients know how much you value their referrals to ensure repeat business. Keeping in contact by sending cards, newsletters, emails, or phone calls. Generally speaking, it's better to remind your clients how much you appreciate their referrals and repeat business, *after* you have proven your value. This will be best demonstrated by the successful close of escrow.

As a final note, remember that while you may work very hard and have ensured the successful close of escrow, don't think that a client will not remember a call that was not returned, an inconvenience you caused that could have been avoided, or impatience on your part that became evident in your communications with the client. They remember everything.

Communication Skills Summary

Understanding the emotional and financial stresses buying or selling a home presents will take you far in learning to empathize and communicate well with your clients and prospective clients. Recognizing and working with the various obstacles that sometimes surface will help you to develop strategies and gain insight so that you are always prepared for whatever lies ahead.

Professional Profile

Betty Plashal
Bplashal@aol.com
Long and Foster, Sterling, Virginia
Years in Business: 29

"Real estate problems most often deal with just two things- time and money. These kinds of problems can always be solved with good negotiating skills. If for some reason a real estate transaction falls apart- forget it, put it in the past and then just go forward with new transactions. Use the bad experiences as a good learning source."

Professional Profile

Brenda Ghibaudy
Ghibaudy@gate.net
RE/MAX, Fort Lauderdale, Florida
Years in Business: 18

"Always listen to your clients very carefully. Show them how much you care not how much you know."

Working with buyers and sellers requires effective communication skills above all else. Much of which, as we have already stated, involves listening. You will need to cultivate good listening and speaking skills, the ability to overcome objections and offer necessary counseling and reassurance, and certainly the ability to remain calm, regardless of the situation.

Professional Profile
Janet Van Zile
Janetvanzile@sprintmail.com
Allen Tate Company, Charlotte, North Carolina
Years in Business: 8

"Listening is a top priority when working with clients. Very often a difficult client only needs someone to listen and show them both sides of the issue. Always, the Golden Rule works in real estate issues- practice it."

To close this never ending always growing topic of client communications and customer service, it is important to remember that your clients are the basis of the real estate business and that *everyone* you meet is a prospective client. With this in mind, it is crucial that you develop your customer service and listening skills. You will also want to refrain from overreacting to people and situations that will not be improved upon as a result of such behavior. People first, property second, the end goals always in mind!

WHAT CONSUMERS WANT

A randomly selected group of homebuyers and sellers were asked what kinds of things they looked for in a real estate professional. While most of the aforementioned material reflects these needs fairly well, it is still interesting to consider the consumer's perspective.

It's important to remember that while you are working hard behind the scenes to market the property, working with the lender, filling out the forms, and the myriad of other tasks that must be accomplished in order to effectively sell and list properties, the client isn't seeing much. From the consumer's point of view, often times, the negotiations, efforts, and time a REALTOR® spends goes unnoticed. The irony is that this is precisely how it should work; the seller isn't supposed to worry that you're scrambling to pull a deal together, only that you did indeed manage to get the escrow closed.

This being the case, it's critical to your customer service skills to understand that the client can and will judge you and your efforts primarily on what it is they see or hear first hand. Here are the top two concerns that buyers and sellers noted:

COMMUNICATIONS/FOLLOW UP

Homeowners and buyers want to know what's going on. We're living in the age of information and the absolute worst thing you can do to your client is leave them in the dark.

Even if you have no news to tell your client or prospect, call them! Most people would rather be kept in the loop than to sit there wondering what is going on. This is especially true when it involves something as important as real estate. For listings, even if there is no action, it's important that you constantly keep in contact with your sellers. Let them know what other activity is going on in the neighborhood. Fill them in on what measures you're taking to sell their property. Most importantly, give them a sense of security in the fact that you are there, working hard to sell their home.

For buyers, let them know each time a new listing (that meets their requirements) goes on the market. Also, it's good to let them know what kind of activity has been going on in the areas that appeal to them. Keeping them apprised of the fact that acreage is going up in price in a certain part of town, will arm them with the information they'll need to make a wise purchasing decision.

Generally speaking, people simply want to know what's going on, and moreover, that you haven't forgotten about them or quit working for them. While the frequency of contacts may vary with your own clients and prospects, a once a week contact is a good rule of thumb. This, of course, is assuming that there is no other reason for which you might want to contact them even more often. Keeping the lines of communication open with your clients is paramount to your customer service skills. A simple phone call that lets them know you are still there, working for their best interests, can take you a long way in their eyes.

Consumer Perspective

Alice Rumbaugh
Resident of Sacramento, California
Number of Homes Purchased: 11
Number of Homes Sold: 10

What do you look for in a REALTOR?

"Someone I can trust to follow through, get me the best possible deal, look out for my best interests, and keep me informed through all phases of the transaction. When I go to buy a house, I want all the information the REALTOR® can get me to assist me in my purchasing decision."

HONESTY/ETHICS

Both buyers and sellers expect to work with honest and ethical real estate professionals. While this seems as if it is something that might go without saying, it is interesting to note what a big concern this tends to be with the general home buying and selling public.

Clearly real estate sales involves large amounts of money, and even the most trusting homeowner is justified in his concern to work with someone who is keeping his best interest in mind. It is easy to understand how buyers and sellers feel might feel vulnerable when their life savings and/or personal assets are on the line.

While we've already established the fact that in order to be a REALTOR®, it is essential that you abide by the highest code of ethics imaginable. You must also remember how your actions appear to others. For example, if you are in favor of your seller accepting an offer because you recognize the benefits of an all cash deal, make sure you explain exactly how and why this is a benefit to the seller. In the same vein, if your experience and expertise leads you to believe a property might sell for higher or lower than what the seller is thinking, tell them why.

In more cases than not, the minute of doubt occurs when honest and ethical people fail to clarify their actions. This is not meant to imply that this, or any other industry, is free from unethical individuals. It , however, meant to demonstrate that all REALTORS® must pay close attention to the actions, words, and message they put forth to their clients. Extra special effort should always be extended when communicating with buyers and sellers so that they are constantly aware of what is happening and why. Couple that with your own industry experience and expertise and then share what you know. You will always be considered highly ethical if you conduct yourself in this manner.

It would be untrue to act as if the commission check didn't count. By being upfront and forthright and making sure your client knows that their best interest is your priority, you will earn a reputation as an honest and ethical REALTOR® who cares. This alone will dramatically improve your business.

COMMUNICATING BEYOND THE CLIENT

"I feel that if a person has problems communicating the very least he can do is to shut up."

Tom Lehrer

Other Agents

Real estate selling careers entail communications that span well beyond those you will have with your clients. Client communications certainly are critical to your success, but there are also other key players in the real estate game who you will need to communicate with on a daily basis. As we have already noted, the relationship you have with your broker will be an important one, as well as the relationships you will develop with other agents. In addition to the other agents who work in your office, you will also enter many transactions with agents who may or may not work in your office and who are representing the buyer or seller in a transaction. This is what we mean when we refer to "other agents." Numerous agents around the country have noted how important, and sometimes frustrating, the relationship with other agents can be. This is why it is so important to recognize the critical nature this relationship represents, and then to act accordingly.

> *Professional Profile*
> Trudy Ault
> Trudyault@REALTOR.com
> Rhoades Realty, Incorporated, Fort Collins, Colorado
> Years in Business: 9
>
> "All new REALTORS® need to realize that fellow agents are co-workers. Buyers and sellers come and go, but the other agents are the ones you constantly do business with, treat them with respect."

If you sell real estate in a highly populated city or state, you might enter into transactions with different agents often. Whereas, if you operate your business in a smaller community or more rural area, you might know just about all the REALTORS® in town. Either way, eventually, you'll catch on to the fact that you belong to a very specialized community; a REALTOR® community. The reasons you joined your local, state, and national associations are the same reasons you learn to communicate effectively with your fellow agents: you are a professional. This is not to imply that all of your communications with other agents, affiliates, or clients, will be completely free of frustration. Understand that this is a highly competitive industry, but competitiveness need not breed contempt.

When you're dependent upon closed transactions and commission checks for your very survival, it is easy to see how such motivation might propel you forward. The point is that it's not necessary in your drive to succeed to run over those who stand in your path. There are more buyers and sellers than there are REALTORS®, and it is always better to win a listing or a sale on your own merits, competition or not.

Professional Profile

Professional Profile
Laura E. Shifrin
Tcr_laurie@net1plus.com
Townsend Center Realty, Incorporated, Townsend, Massachusetts
Years in Business: 23

"Look like number one and you will be number one. Work well with your competitors, no matter what...it will pay in the long run."

The first step in working well with other agents is to gain a clear perspective on the situation and then to apply the communication technique discussed earlier. Other REALTORS® are much like you. They are energetic, enthusiastic, skilled and talented people who enjoy selling and listing homes. Also like you, they work for a broker (or are a broker), pay taxes, buy groceries, and try hard to pull deals together. Hopefully, like you too, they are a part of organized real estate and recognize the value of their professional associations. Finally, and probably the most important tip to remember, they want the same thing you do; to close the transaction:

Other agents want the same thing you do: to close the transaction

With this simple but accurate understanding, it shouldn't be too difficult to cultivate and appreciate the other agents you come into contact with. There are a few simple rules that will keep your communications and interactions with other agents on a positive note. The first is recognizing that they are, like you, simply trying to sell homes. Even though this basic thought seems somehow esoteric, it isn't. When you look at the other agent in a transaction, act as if you were looking in a mirror, and hope you like what you see!

Showing respect for your fellow agents is a necessity. If you find yourself talking to a potential buyer who walks into an open house you are hosting, and he tells you he's been looking at homes with another agent, but thinks he'd like to write an offer for this one, are you interested? Bite your tongue and put down the pen. As enticing as this might seem, remember the old saying, "what comes around goes around." If another agent has been working hard and following up with a prospective buyer, it is a professional courtesy not to interfere with that relationship. Of course, if the buyer tells you he isn't happy with the other agent and has already told him so, that presents a completely different scenario. This is why buyer-related agreements, acknowledging exclusiveness to one REALTOR®, are beneficial to *all* REALTORS®. The bottom line is this: show the same kind of respect toward other agents as you expect them to show you. You will inevitably be rewarded.

Your communication skills and techniques are equally important to apply to other agents. When two REALTORS® are working together on the same transaction, one representing the buyer and one the seller, it is important to remember that the end goal is the same-even if occasionally it doesn't appear so. For that very reason, it is vital to keep the end goal in mind at all times and if necessary, to remind the other agent of the merits and rewards of that goal. In addition, recall that everyone is human and that even you, yes you, have made mistakes or forgotten to do something you said you would do. So in addition to the effective communication skills we have already discussed, when working with other agents, you might need to remember that you're both in the same proverbial boat. The interaction that results has a fairly significant impact on both sets of clients.

In order to give you a specific example of how to gear your communications and your thought process in a manner that is more conducive to an effective outcome, let's look at a classic example of how this theory can be applied. Then, we will follow with a list of the most common complaints, or areas of contention, that REALTORS® across the nation noted to be their pet peeves when working with other agents.

You've worked diligently to close the sale of your buyer's new home. You've made arrangements with the other agent to drop off the key the afternoon of closing and your buyer is arriving with the moving van at 5:00 p.m. You've told the buyer the key will be in the mailbox. Surprise. The call comes in. You detect an obvious note of frustration that borders on panic in your buyer's otherwise calm demeanor. She is ready to move into the new home that you've worked so hard to qualify her for, and there's no key. You hang up, after telling her to sit tight, while you contact the other agent. The other agent is at home and completely forgot about the key-he'll be there in twenty minutes.

This doesn't represent the highest form of professionalism. Remember though, REALTORS® are people and sometimes people forget. Try to evaluate these situations on merit, and then act accordingly. In this case, your end goal is to get the buyer her keys, not to spend valuable time criticizing the other agent for his forgetfulness. You will certainly apologize profusely to your buyer, and verify that the keys have arrived in a timely fashion, but in situations like these, is it really fair to say the other agent doesn't know what he's doing?

Often times we let one small error impress our senses to believe someone is something that they are not. Here then it is important to remember that everyone is subject to mistakes and what it really boils down to is intention. If you're dealing with another agent who tells you that your offer is unacceptable and that he refuses to even show it to his seller, that's quite a bit different than a diligent REALTOR® who forgot to drop off a key. Intention is everything and action is the automatic outcome. If and when you do come across the agent who is acting in a way that you do not find compatible with your own set of standards, you must ask yourself, and perhaps your client, how important is this property? If you enter into a transaction with an agent who you do not feel upholds professionalism and high ethics, you will have to work twice as hard to protect your client's interest. You also have the option of never doing business with that agent again, and, if things get really bad, you can always call his broker or place a formal complaint with the Department of Real Estate.

Professional Profile

Joel Goodness
Jgoodlaca@aol.com
Firm: Coldwell Banker, Beverly Hills, California
Years in Business: 3

"It is very important to be honest, not only with other agents, but yourself and your clients! In my Bio on my website, www.goodnessknows.com, I state, *"Your name is the only thing you are born with and in the end, the only thing you take with you…what you do with it, is up to you!"* Most of your work will come from referrals and if you have a good reputation for being honest and fair…it will all fall into place."

Generally speaking though, the kinds of situations you are most likely to incur out in the field, with respect to other agents, are benign. And, in these relatively harmless scenarios, albeit frustrating at the time, it is important to remember to keep your cool and show a little compassion. Effectively communicating in a patient and professional manner is the best thing you can do for your clients. Here is a list of the most common complaints REALTORS® had about other agents who they felt didn't quite make the cut. As you read them, be aware that these are the seemingly small errors you yourself are capable of making. Hopefully this list will arm you with awareness of actions you'll want to avoid:

1) **Not delivering the contract in a timely manner or not wanting to deliver it at all.** Many REALTORS® noted that they found it extremely frustrating when they knew an agent had an offer (a counter offer, an addendum, etc,) but failed to get the contract where it was supposed to be. Perhaps it was too late, the other agent didn't feel like driving all the way "out there," or some other legitimate reason surfaced. It is important to remember that REALTORS® you are working with, or may be entering into a transaction with, are just like you. They expect the same professional standards you do. They don't like holding up the deal or slowing down transactions over forgetfulness, laziness, or other reasons for failure to deliver. Remember that the other agent has a client he is answering to, just like you, and that when you fail to perform your job, it affects everyone. You can count on the fact that if you make the other agent look bad to his clients, you will definitely make yourself look bad to him. If you are in an urgent situation, make arrangements for someone else to deliver the offer-fax it or FedEx it, but get it where it's supposed to be, when it's supposed to be there. This is crucial for establishing your credibility with other REALTORS®.

2) **Not doing what they said they would do.** Here, there were many areas that REALTORS® indicated having problems with. It might be as simple as not delivering a key out of forgetfulness, or something more serious, such as not showing your offer to the seller. Sometimes, in the heat of intense negotiations, it is easy to promise more than you can deliver.

Unfortunately, this is simply not acceptable behavior in the real estate industry. Whether you are trying to secure a listing or negotiating with another REALTOR®, don't promise more than you can comfortably deliver. As a matter of fact, several REALTORS® voluntarily stated:

Promise Less-Deliver More

This saying is worth jotting down and carrying in your briefcase, especially if you tend to be the type that wants to promise the world, just to make everyone feel better. There is no room in real estate transactions for false guarantees. People are investing their time and money in properties and your word is only as good as your action. Don't over promise.

Telling the other agent that you will do something and then not following through guarantees that they will have little faith in your word from that point on. You are trying to establish yourself as a proficient and effective professional and these kinds of mistakes aren't often overlooked. In addition, make sure that you're not the one who is being forgetful. Just because you are sure *you* will remember to: put the key in the mailbox, deliver the guarantee letter, or return a phone call, don't count on it. In a business where your word is as good as gold, or it should be, you can't afford to make careless mistakes. Write it down!

We already noted in the Time Management chapter that you should write down literally everything you need to do. The irony of it is that we tend to think we don't need to write down the seemingly small tasks, and yet it is those small undone tasks that cause deals to crumble. In the business of working with buyers and listing properties, every moment counts, and that's no exaggeration. Here's a small mistake that probably everyone you know has made, yet consider the frustration: You tell another agent that you'll meet him at the property at noon. It has to be exactly at noon because that's when the seller has to leave for an appointment and there is no lockbox. Not to mention, the listing agent has already told you he'll only have ten minutes because he's got to pick up buyers from out of town.

You think you're ready, even if a little rushed, and you head out the door, map-book in hand. Your gas tank reads empty. Sure, you noticed earlier in the day that you needed to fill up, but it was one of "those things." One of those things that you knew you had to do and didn't bother writing it down. Now, since the property you're meeting the other agent at is 20 minutes away and you know the car will only make it 10, you'll need to stop and get gas. The gas station is busy so you have to wait for ten minutes to put enough gas in your car so that you can rush to your appointment. You're late, the seller is mad, and the listing agent looks at you like you're the last person he ever plans on doing business with. He rushes off to pick up his buyers, rolling his eyes at your tardiness. Not a great way to start any transaction, is it? Always write it down and above all, say what you'll do and then do what you say. Always.

Professional Profile

Ted Breden, GRI,CRS,ABR
Ted@affordablehomes.net
Firm: Century 21 Capital Realty, Inc., Chicago, Illinois
Years in Business: 22

"There is more to consider than simply 'getting along' with other agents. The real estate laws of our state demand that we take accountability for our actions to protect the client that we represent in a real estate transaction. It is more than getting along and it is more than a commission; it is instead a responsibility to uphold the fiduciary relationship of the client we were hired to represent."

3) **Not being honest.** Members of organized real estate are under professional obligation to operate under a strict code of ethics. This is a high standard that does not recognize "fibbing" as being an acceptable action, and certainly not outright lying. If an agent delivers an offer that you know your seller will hate, be as honest as possible without betraying your seller's trust, or insulting the other agent. But don't lie, not even for your seller's sake. As a matter of fact, if a client ever asks you to lie, remind him that you are obligated by a higher code of ethics and that you cannot violate them. While out and out lying wasn't an act that REALTORS® noted as being frequent, there were insinuations that often times a little honesty goes along way. Even though your obligation rests primarily with your clients, it is essential that you exhibit an honest and candid mode of communication with all other REALTORS®, at all times. Tell the truth all the time.

4) **Not knowing the business.** It's amazing how many people enter into a business and figure they'll learn along the way. While this may be acceptable in some industries, real estate probably isn't one of them. Sure, you can start selling and listing properties left and right, but you'd better know the laws, contracts, and practices of what you're doing. If you're just starting out, make sure you take classes, read books, and study forms. Also, understand the specific laws, such as disclosures, set backs, and city or county ordinances that might affect your dealings. And even then, confirm with your broker, mentor, or other established agent, that you're doing what needs to be done. When people are buying or selling houses, a lot is on the line, often times someone's life savings. Patience for beginners who aren't educating themselves is not well tolerated. An experienced REALTOR® who receives a contract not properly completed, or sees actions not consistent with the business, will automatically note a red flag next to your name. Show respect to those already established in the industry, as well as to the buyers and sellers you'll be impacting. Know your business. If you don't, ask someone who does. Keep current on the laws and practices and strive to be proficient in your industry.

5) **Not being nice.** Generally speaking, REALTORS® are jovial kinds of characters. Enthusiastic, outgoing, and people-oriented. However, we are all subject to bad days. It will do you well if you look upon other

agents as extended clients. Consider this scenario, which many an established REALTOR® will recognize: Your seller has just spent 20 minutes complaining that he doesn't want to pay $1500 for dry rot damage and that you'd better find another way to pay for it, or else the deal is off. At times like these, it's not always easy to keep a cool head. You've read between the lines, kept your end goal in mind, and tried hard to stay calm but the problem hasn't gone away. You get off the phone and call the other agent.

Remember when you communicate with the other agent, to think of this person as an extended client. Treat him or her with the same degree of courtesy, respect, and patience you would your customers. How you handle this communication has an impact on more than just this single transaction. If you blow up at the other agent because the seller has upset you, you are pulling yourself even further from the immediate goal of resolving the dry rot issue. The other agent wants the same thing as you do-to close the transaction. The other agent is representing his client the same as you are representing your own. Together, with sharp, honest, and creative negotiation skills, the two of you can come up with a plan that is agreeable to both buyer and seller and to each of you. It's all about courteous communications.

Professional Profile

Dick Rubright
dick@shermanco.com
Broker-Associate, Sherman and Company REALTORS®, Kerrville, Texas
Years in Business: 30

"Lend a hand to any struggling peer, for in helping, you reinforce your knowledge and improve your image as a caring person. Be proud of your profession because you can and WILL make a difference."

The well-known rules for working with other agents involve honest, forthright, respectful, and constant communications (keeping the other agent informed as to any occurrence that may affect the deal, returning phone calls), and doing what you say you'll do. If you tell the other agent you'll deliver the offer at 5:00 p.m., then deliver the offer at 5:00 p.m. If you say you'll leave the keys in the mailbox, then leave the keys in the mailbox. These may appear to be seemingly simple and glaringly obvious, but unfortunately, these are the exact actions that cause bad blood between fellow agents.

Professional Profile

Laura E. Shifrin

Tcr_laurie@net1plus.com

Townsend Center Realty, Incorporated, Townsend, MA

Years in Business: 23

"Look like number one and you will be number one. Work well with your competitors no matter what- it will pay in the long run."

Probably the single most helpful tip anyone could give you on the merits of working well with other agents is this:

Treat other REALTORS® with the same respect, honesty, and ethical behavior as you do your clients-
as a matter of fact-think of them as extended clients

Recognize that your obligation as a REALTOR® is to provide the most outstanding representation to your clients, and that other agents have the same *exact* obligation to their clients. There is absolutely no reason under the sun that you both can't accomplish these goals while simultaneously exhibiting integrity and professional courtesy. With honest and effective communication skills, smart negotiations, and a mutually extended respect for all parties involved, there are very few things that can stand in the way of a successful transaction. It's all about working together and communicating well.

Communication Work Sheets

Because effective communications will be so important to your ultimate success in real estate sales, take time now to identify your triggers. Your triggers are those things that you tend to react to. By training yourself to keep a look out for potential problems, you're well on your way to overcome communication obstacles before they surface.

Remember that it takes time to perfect your communication skills, and that practice makes perfect. These exercises have been designed to assist you in understanding the most effective way to communicate, in spite of triggers, conflicts, or misunderstandings. The sample scenarios are intentionally geared toward situations that might normally cause you to react negatively, so that you can begin to analyze and plan a more effective response.

In order for these exercises to be truly effective, telling the truth is key. Be brutally honest when asked your first reaction, regardless of how negative, immature, or unprofessional it may seem. Getting the automatic emotional reaction out of your system often helps to clear the way for more productive work. While we all know how to bite our tongue and say the professionally correct thing when needed, these exercises will minimize the frustration those challenging confrontations tends to present. This is done by reminding ourselves to keep our communication efforts in direct alignment with our goals.

Remember, the key to effective communications always involves listening to what's being said, as well as what isn't.

✪ IDENTIFY YOUR GOALS

Ask yourself what the **end-goal** is-what are you ultimately after? It usually is related to closing the transaction. Next, ask yourself what the immediate goal, or **mini-goal** is-what needs to happen right now to get you back on track with your end-goal? Remember that both the end-goal and mini-goal should be directly related to maintaining the relation-ship and ensuring repeat or referral business.

✪ LISTEN

People need to be heard. Listen and repeat back what you hear. Help the other person clarify what they are saying to you by telling them what they said. Another important component to listening is to hear what the other person *isn't* saying. Probe, hear more than just their words. You role is to help them successfully solve the problem. Use your ears.

✪ EMPATHIZE

Put yourself in their shoes. Remember that people get scared, have bad days, and sometimes feel threatened. If you think about being the other person, and then imagine why they might be feeling the way they do, you are that much closer to resolving the issue from a point of understanding.

✪ RESPOND EFFECTIVELY

If you've followed all the steps above, responding effectively should be fairly easy. Before you speak, ask yourself the following questions:

- Is this taking me closer to my goals?
- Have I listened to what this person is saying?
- Have I tried to understand how they feel?
- What can I say that will help to resolve the issue?

Now respond, and notice how the whole world opens up for those who practice effective communications skills. Not only will you be better equipped to handle difficult situations, comfort clients, and overcome obstacles, you will also be ensuring that referral and repeat business finds it way back to you!

Communication Exercises

Exercise 1

Situation: Your seller has just called you and said his wife wants to take the house off the market because she thinks next year will be a better time to sell.

Your IMMEDIATE reaction would be: (don't hold back, let it roll)

_____

_____

_____

_____

_____

_____

STOP!
What is your long-term goal?

_____

_____

What is your immediate/mini-goal?

_____

_____

_____

What might this person be thinking, worried about, or afraid of right now?

_____

_____

_____

_____

_____

What is the EFFECTIVE response? (words that will bring you closer to the goals noted above, while identifying and addressing the real issues that may exist)

_____

_____

_____

_____

_____

_____

_____

_____

_____

_____

_____

_____

Exercise 2

Situation: Your buyer just informed you that she thinks the mortgage might be too high for her and she would like to rescind her offer (you suspect her mother helped "convince" her)

Your IMMEDIATE reaction would be: (don't hold back, let it roll)

_____

_____

_____

_____

_____

_____

STOP!
What is your long-term goal?

_____

_____

What is your immediate/mini-goal?

_____

_____

What might this person be thinking, worried about, or afraid of right now?

_____

_____

_____

_____

_____

What's the EFFECTIVE response? (what will bring you closer to the goals noted above, while identifying and addressing other issues that might exist)

_____

_____

_____

_____

_____
_____
_____
_____
_____
_____
_____

Exercise 3

Situation: The listing agent told you that he would drop off the counter offer and so far, he's two hours late. Finally, after you've turned out the lights, he shows up at the door.

Your IMMEDIATE reaction would be: (don't hold back, let it roll)

_____
_____
_____
_____
_____
_____
_____

STOP!
What is your long-term goal?

_____
_____

What is your immediate/mini-goal?

_____
_____
_____

What might this person be thinking, worried about, or afraid of right now?

_____
_____
_____
_____
_____
_____

What's the EFFECTIVE response? (what will bring you closer to the goals noted above, while identifying and addressing other issues that may exist)

_____
_____
_____
_____
_____
_____
_____
_____
_____
_____
_____

Exercise 4

Situation: Your buyer from last year called and told you that the roof is leaking (on a house you sold her a year ago) and what are you going to do about it.

Your IMMEDIATE reaction would be: (don't hold back, let it roll)

_____
_____
_____

_____

_____

_____

_____

STOP!

What is your long-term goal?

_____

_____

What is your immediate/mini-goal?

_____

_____

What might this person be thinking, worried about, or afraid of right now?

_____

_____

_____

_____

_____

What's the EFFECTIVE response? (what will bring you closer to the goals noted above, while identifying and addressing other issues that might exist)

_____

_____

_____

_____

_____

_____

_____

_____

_____

_____

_____

_____

_____

Exercise 5 Now it's your turn!

Use these next two pages to create scenarios that contain your individual triggers and pre-determine how you're going to handle them in a manner that conducive to keeping the deal together and helping you accomplish your goals.

Situation:

_____

_____

_____

_____

_____

Your IMMEDIATE reaction would be: (don't hold back, let it roll)

_____

_____

_____

_____

_____

_____

STOP!
What is your long-term goal?

_____

_____

_____

What is your immediate/mini-goal?

_____

_____

_____

What might this person be thinking, worried about, or afraid of right now?

_____

_____

_____

_____

_____

_____

What's the EFFECTIVE response? (what will bring you closer to the goals noted above, while identifying and addressing other issues that may exist)

_____

_____

_____

_____

_____

_____

_____

_____

Exercise 6

Situation:

_____

_____

_____

_____

_____

_____

Your IMMEDIATE reaction would be: (don't hold back, let it roll)

_____

_____

_____

_____

_____

_____

STOP!
What is your long-term goal?

_____

_____

What is your immediate/mini-goal?

_____

_____

What might this person be thinking, worried about, or afraid of right now?

_____

_____

_____

_____

_____

What's the EFFECTIVE response? (what will bring you closer to the goals noted above, while identifying and addressing the real issues above)

_____

_____

_____

AFFILIATES ARE YOUR FRIENDS

Now that we've covered communications and interactions with clients and other agents, it's time to consider those external forces that can make or break a real estate deal, affiliates. They are also known as service providers. Affiliates come in many varieties, and there are some whose services are more crucial and common than others, but ultimately, each affiliate is like the corner piece of a complex puzzle, without it, the picture isn't complete.

Understanding what's involved, and establishing strong working relationships with a host of affiliates is important. Realizing that the affiliate's goal is the same as yours-to close real estate transactions-helps you gain a better understanding that they indeed are trying to do the same job you are, only in this case, you're as much the client as the buyer or seller is. Building affiliate relationships is vital to your professional success.

Professional Profile

Don Sheets
Wesellcvg@aol.com
Huff Realty, Cincinnati, Ohio
Years in Business: 6

"Develop a strong support network early on. Work with only a couple of loan processors, home inspectors, handymen, etc. The best loan rate or repair quote doesn't always mean the best service and outcome. Good familiar working relationships will help to avoid many unexpected problems and further your career and reputation as a professional who takes care of clients."

To give you a better perspective and somewhat of a sampling of what will be involved in virtually all of your real estate transactions, we've provided some inside-insight from two of the most common and frequently relied upon affiliates; lenders and title companies.

Working With Lenders

Lenders are the ones responsible for providing the funds so that buyers can purchase homes. If you are working with a buyer, you will want to be sure that your lender can assist with pre-approval financing.

Professional Profile

Dave Holmes
Holmesrealty@msn.com
RE/MAX Greater Atlanta, Atlanta Georgia
Years in Business: 5

"It really helps to take a mortgage class and be fully involved in the loan process with your clients along the way."

In an effort to offer more enlightenment into the seemingly mysterious land of loans, we worked with COUNTRYWIDE mortgage to find out what kinds of things a REALTOR® should be aware of in the ever-evolving world of real estate lending.

Interview With a Lender

Countrywide Home Loans, Inc.
http://REALTORS.countrywide.com/
Mike Taliaferro, executive vice president
Plano, Texas 375 branches nationwide, More than 10,000 employees

Explain the primary role a lender plays in the real estate transaction.

A mortgage lender handles everything related to finances during a home
purchase transaction. This includes:

- pre-approving potential homebuyers so that they know how much home
  they can afford before they begin to shop;
- educating homebuyers on their financing options and the loan
  application process;
- helping homebuyers gather the paperwork necessary to begin the
  application and underwriting process;
- explaining the forms that are integral to the transaction and assisting
  homebuyers with interpreting and completing the paperwork correctly;
- keeping the homebuyer apprised of the status of the loan and working
  with them to expedite the process; and
- explaining the closing process and coordinating the required closing
  services, such as property appraisal, title search and insurance, flood
  certification, and other services provided by vendors.

The lender is an advisor all through the process and should be available to
answer any and all questions. Frequently the lender also serves as a
facilitator in the process, providing expedited service to help process
delayed paperwork, or helping to identify resources such as reliable
insurance providers that can underwrite a homeowners policy or home
warranty quickly in order to meet closing deadlines.

*How do REALTORS® learn about the various kinds of loan programs
available?*

REALTORS® most often learn about available loan programs through their
established relationship with a mortgage lender. They may also attend
training workshops provided by lenders and receive direct mail and/or e-
mails that fill them in on the latest trends in lending. Increasingly,
REALTORS® also take advantage of lending information available online

consumers expect. Lenders that offer a broad variety of loan products and innovative loan features can better meet the needs of diverse clients. Also, lenders who strive to meet the specific needs of growing cultural groups will be helpful as the demographics of the average homebuyer change over time.

Obviously, the lender's track record for performance and integrity is extremely important. Particularly in hot real estate markets or periods of low housing inventory, it's vital that a lender be able to process and close a loan quickly. Excellent customer service is also important; discourteous, unprofessional or inefficient service can sour a client's experience and reflect unfavorably on the referring REALTOR®.

Is "lender loyalty" (sticking primarily with one lender) a good rule of thumb for REALTORS® to remember?

Developing a strong relationship with one or a few lenders offers some distinct advantages. It allows the REALTOR® to gain greater understanding of specific lenders' loan offerings, and to develop a greater degree of confidence in the lender's services. Real estate transactions are often complex, high-pressure, and emotionally charged, so having an established relationship with a lender can certainly help smooth and speed the financing side of the process. While any good lending professional should be willing to "go the extra mile" to deliver financing, a personal relationship and repeat referrals are powerful motivators for exceptional service.

Realistically, the pressures and work volume that most REALTORS® juggle don't allow them the luxury of constantly identifying, checking and comparing various lenders. Therefore, working with one or a few solid, reputable lenders helps REALTORS® give clients good financing referrals while letting them focus on the core customer service and marketing functions of their jobs.

Why is it so important to pre-qualify buyers and what does it involve?

There are several reasons that pre-qualification is extremely important to a smooth and successful real estate transaction:

- It establishes a realistic target price range for the buyer, which avoids the disappointment of falling in a love with a property that is unattainable, as well as the possibility of excluding more expensive homes that may in fact be affordable.

Consumers are sometimes confused by the terms "pre-qualification" and "pre-approval." A buyer who submits very basic financial information receives a pre-qualification that signifies *only* that the lender estimates the amount the buyer might be eligible for, based on the information provided. To obtain pre-approval, a buyer provides more detailed financial information and grants the lender permission to pull a credit report and verify income. Because the lender has sufficient information to assess credit risk, it can provide a more accurate estimate of the precise loan amount the buyer qualifies for, and issue a pre-approval that assures the buyer can receive that loan, subject to property appraisal and no changes in the information that was previously provided.

What other services can lenders provide that might be helpful for REALTORS® to know?

Countrywide has a profound appreciation for REALTORS® as valued business partners. We've developed a complete online resource center tailored to their needs, called REALTOR® Advantage (http://REALTORS.countrywide.com). The site provides tailored access to information on Countrywide's loan products, free registration in our national online directory of real estate professionals, upfront approvals online, and Lock N' Sell rate protection that helps listing agents give buyers a convenient financing option. Plus, we offer REALTORS® who complete the free registration additional benefits, including a monthly real estate TRENDS newsletter, and a month's free membership and online continuing education credits through isucceed.com.

What information can some lenders provide that helps REALTORS® in their business?

We have a host of tools and a wide array of information that can help move nervous or undecided prospects into committed buyers. Some examples:
- Calculators that help prospects see the potential savings and tax benefits of buying versus renting.
- An affordability calculator that helps potential buyers assess how much they may be able to afford for monthly payments.
- Information on the loan process, to take some of the fear and uncertainty out of what is an anxiety-producing and intimidating process.

Professional Profile

Jo Ann Hatfield
Joannhatfield@grar.com
Village Belles Real Estate, Incorporated, Grand Rapids, Michigan
Years in Business: 5

"There's a program for FHA buyers called Neimiah, which I knew nothing about, but there are lots of things you need to be aware of: new roof guarantee, home warranty, etc. As it turned out, we almost lost the deal, but fortunately, and thanks to a good lender, myself, and the other agent, we were able to pull things together. Work with your lender and know all about the programs he or she offers."

Working With Title/Escrow

In addition to developing an excellent working relationship with a lender you can count on, you'll also need to find a good place to close those escrows. Some states combine title and escrow, and some do not. For our purposes here, we'll combine title and escrow as one process with two parts, recognizing that in some areas or states, they may be part of two completely separate entities.

Professional Profile

Courtney Self
Courtney@self.cc.com
RE/MAX Executives, Redondo Beach, California
Years in Business: 14

"I started my own networking group of local professionals, with the help of my title representative and my lender. We now have about twelve members and I have closed about five transactions as a direct result of this group or referrals from this group. The cost was minimal and we've all made new friends."

In order to provide you with a better understanding as to the overall tasks the title people perform in an effort to close each escrow successfully, we talked to FIRST AMERICAN TITLE; a large company serving many parts of the United States.

Understanding Title Insurance

First American Title Insurance Company (a subsidiary of First American Corporation)
Size: 800 Branches and approximately 5,000 agents/13,000 employees
Location: Throughout the United States and Canada, Australia, United Kingdom, the Caribbean, and more.

First American Title traces its roots to 1889, in Santa Ana, California. In order to give you a bird's-eye perspective on what the title industry is all about, we spoke with **Albert Rush, S.V.P./National Counsel**, Santa Ana, California. brush@firstam.com

Explain the role of title representative.

"The title representative introduces customers and potential customers to our products and services, and to local employees and agents who are there to service customers' needs. The representative also troubleshoots customers' orders, when needed."

Why is title and escrow so important and what exactly does it mean?

"The importance of title and escrow calls for a very lengthy answer. Understand that escrow is the process of closing a real estate transaction. Escrow involves getting and recording releases of paid-off liens and mortgages, getting and recording deeds, handling pay-offs, getting and recording deed of trust and mortgage documents ("docs"), and satisfying other seller/buyer/lender needs in connection with closing the transaction. Title insurance in many ways insures the escrow and closing process."
To give anyone who is interested a more technical response, I suggest looking at our website, www.firstam.com/ look for "Archive/Reference"/look for "Claims Chronicles." Also on the Welcome Page look for "Archive/Reference"/look for "Buyer/Seller Information." Then, look for "Q&A Title Insurance for the Property Owner" and "70 Something Ways to Lose Your Property." These will explain what is covered and why it is so important to have title insurance."

Why should REALTORS® worry about getting to know a representative prior to having any deals to close?

"It's important to establish a relationship with a reputable escrow/title company to make sure real estate transactions in which they are interested are handled competently, promptly, with a minimum of hassles, and with the best insurance coverage and service ultimately provided to the parties."

What kinds of services are offered to REALTORS®?

"All sorts of services are provided for REALTORS®, including property profiles (as permitted by law), escrow services, title insurance, and related products- this applies to both buyers and sellers. A REALTOR® should ask their sales representative for additional services and details of those services."

What should REALTORS® looks for in a title company?

"Agents (REALTORS®), will want to find a title representative/escrow person who can answer their questions, help facilitate transaction, and can be responsive to their needs. They want to work with someone knowledgeable enough to make things run smoothly, and reputable enough to best protect the interest of all parties in the transaction, reducing the likelihood of disagreements, misunderstandings, callbacks, and litigation."

As for locating affiliates, this is generally not a problem. As a REALTOR®, you will often find your office mail slot exploding with flyers and handouts advertising a barrage of real estate-related services. The choices for virtually every kind of service will be ten fold. Until you have been in the industry long enough to acquire a sixth sense about who does what they say they will do, you'll want to ask other REALTORS® which affiliates they've worked with and what their experiences have been. Remember though, ask more than one agent, as everyone has different opinions and measures effectiveness in different ways. You wouldn't want to deny yourself or your clients the service of a superior company because one REALTOR® you know had an unfortunate experience.

Professional Profile
Caroline Bianchi, CBR, GRI, LTG
Cbian17435@aol.com
RE/MAX Acclaim, Auburn, Massachusetts
Years in Business:

"Your clients must trust you and in order to achieve that, you must be able to educate them on the mortgage, inspection, broker, and closing components of each transaction. These companies consist of key people who will enable the client to move through the transaction without feeling overwhelmed."

Different states require the use of different kinds of affiliates. If you live in Florida, you may require a hurricane disclosure; in California, earthquake, and in Texas, tornados. The important thing to learn from this is that whatever the requirements in your particular state or region happen to be, they must be met by professional, reputable affiliates. These are the professionals who you are entrusting to help close your real estate transactions. Don't send your client to a lender you wouldn't use yourself, or order repairs from a handyman who you wouldn't let touch a shingle on your own home.

Recognize that affiliates must generate business from REALTORS®, just as you need to generate the business of prospective buyers and sellers. Here is list of potential affiliates you may want to establish a relationship with, at least to the extent of an informal interview. That way, when the time is ready to call upon their services, you'll be prepared.

- Lenders
- Title /Escrow Companies
- Disclosure Companies
- Pest Control Services
- Real Estate Attorney
- Appraiser

- Home Inspection Company
- Home Warranty Company
- Home Repair (handyman) Service
- Painters, Roofers, Landscapers, etc.

Rather than making a mistake at your client's expense, it is always wise to do your homework. As mentioned earlier, ask around. Once you have established a good working relationship with particular affiliates, it is wise to demonstrate the same kind of unwavering loyalty you expect of your own clients. Remember, affiliates are your friends and working for the same goal you are: to successfully close real estate transactions!

Use the following page to record those service providers you use, notes about their services you want to remember, and contact information.

Service Provider Contact List and Notes

Name/Service	Contact Person	Telephone/Email

NOTES:_____

TECHNOLOGY

"If you do not think about the future, you cannot have one."
John Galsworthy

Interview With the President

Richard A. Mendenhall, CIPS, CRB, GRI

RE/MAX Boone Realty, Columbia Missouri- Owner/120+ REALTORS

Years in Business: 27

President 2001 National Association of REALTORS®

How do you see technology changing the industry?

"It will bring a multitude of new real estate business models to the market, some which will stick and many won't."

Do you think it's true that REALTORS® of all ages are jumping on the "technology band wagon" and do you think it's critical that they do become computer literate?

"Yes. But so far, I think only about one third of the REALTORS® are on the bandwagon. With 40% of the consumers already on the net, it will drive REALTORS to learn computer technology too."

What else can you tell us about technology?

"Here's a concept that has my attention: What drives consumer E-loyalty is, 65% quality of customer support, 58% on time delivery, 49% product representation, 24% information, 23% site design and navigation, and 19% price. Not long ago no one owned a single square inch of the earth; today someone owns every square inch of it. Someday soon, the same will be said of the Internet."

Technology in the real estate industry is an on going trend. Quite clearly, an entire book could be (and surely has been) written on this single subject alone. Technology is always evolving, even to the extent that new things have probably emerged since the time this sentence was written. You'll have to take steps to ensure that you are consistently up to speed. Technology can be an incredible boon to your real estate career, but will require some effort on your part. There are new kinds of software and technologies that will continue to streamline the real estate industry, and yes, there will come a time in the near future when complete transactions will take place over the Internet. For now, let's concentrate on the basics and how they can contribute to your business.

For the sake of clarity, we will focus upon the advantages of three particular areas of technology that are sure to impact the way you work: equipment, the Internet, and software. This basic overview will provide you with an introduction, as well as an insight on which technologies you are interested in pursuing and learning more about.

Equipment in this sense will not merely be limited to computers. Today's REALTOR® depends upon an entire host of equipment beyond the computer room and we will touch, at least lightly upon some of these technology related products. The Internet opens many doors for successful agents. In addition to the ever-increasing e-commerce possibilities, there are online listing opportunities and REALTOR® websites, email marketing, and real estate resources. The Internet presents ample business opportunities that smart REALTORS® will learn to take immediate advantage of.

Finally, software abounds in the real estate industry. Just go to any real estate trade show or convention and you'll be swept away by the abundance of new software products hitting the shelves everyday. While this section is not intended to give you specific direction in which products to buy, there are a few innovative solutions that every agent should be aware of, such as electronic forms and contact management software. Please note that Appendixes provides more detailed product and tool information, as well as a list of web resources that includes many of the web site addresses for products and technologies you will read about in this chapter. In addition to your own research and interests, it is always helpful to speak to technology-savvy REALTORS® whose advice you can rely on, as well as your broker, for keeping current on the latest and greatest trends in real estate technology.

EQUIIPMENT

As we enter a new era of technological advancements, electronic gadgets prevail, including those you will use in relation to your daily activities. Before we delve more deeply into the basic and necessary technology equipment that you will use along with your computer, let's take a quick look at mobile-commerce, otherwise known as m-commerce.

Mobile commerce includes cell phones, pagers, blackberries, and even computerized mapping programs that will lead you to properties simply for the asking. Of these, most REALTORS® acknowledge that the cell phone is relied on the most. Cell phones truly are crucial for the busy sales associate who spends much of her time on the road. You wouldn't want to miss an important call from your lender, or a lead from a prospective client because you happen to be away from your office. There are many cell phones available today with too many features to mention. There are new wireless cell phones that truly mark the era of mobile commerce by downloading your email and giving you driving directions—the list goes on.

Ask other REALTORS® which brands of cell phones, with which features, they use and speak to different dealers about the various programs that exist. If your experience with cell phones is limited, please note that there is a significant difference in the original investment you'll make for a cell phone versus the on-going service charge. Service providers are forever featuring promotions and sales that offer reasonable rates and discounted or extended hours. As a busy and productive REALTOR®, you will certainly want to track down the most cost-effective and high-performing cell phone available. Remember too, even the most careful driver can be easily distracted when negotiating big deals, or even dialing telephone numbers, while on the road. Always practice safety and use your common sense when conducting business on the road.

Professional Profile

John Ryley, Broker/Vice President
jryley@coldwellbanker.com
Coldwell Banker Hunt Kennedy & Cranford, Brooklyn, New York
Office in Business: 30 years

"This is rapidly becoming a technology business. The consumer can now get stock quotes and make trades on a palm pilot, or cell phone. They want and expect the same level of information in a real estate transaction."

In addition to mobile capabilities, you'll need easy access to a good copy and fax machine. Even though many computers today feature internal fax programs, unless you are using electronic forms, which we will cover soon, you'll need a fax machine. Your broker will supply you with a photocopy and fax machine in the office, but if you plan on working out of your home, make sure you have easy access to this kind of dependable equipment. Now on to computers...

Computer technology is changing every moment and it would be literally impossible to note the top of the line computer at this specific reading, as it will most certainly change momentarily. Fortunately, there are many well-known reputable computer stores staffed with knowledgeable technology-minded sales crews that will guide you through this often confusing purchase. Here, we will note the basic requirements to run most programs and some of the optional components that might suit your needs. For hardware basics, we talked to Albert Tran, Software Manager for the California Association of REALTORS®.

Technology: Basic Equipment

Albert Tran
Albert_Tran@car.org
Software Manager, California Association of REALTORS®
Masters in Computer Science, Licensed Real Estate Broker
Los Angeles, California

"For doing real estate business online, the most important piece of equipment is your computer. Other hardware, such as scanner, digital camera, modem, and monitor, can be essential, too. You do not have to spend a fortune to invest on computer hardware. Please remember your computer might become outdated in just a few years. Before purchasing a computer, I like to recommend REALTORS® shop around for an affordable one by checking with various electronic stores.

Ideally, your computer should have the following items: a Processor, RAM (Random Access Memory), a Hard Disk Storage, a CD-ROM drive, a Floppy Drive, a Mouse, a Keyboard, a Modem, and a pair of Speakers. In order to run basic and real estate related software, and operate effectively, I usually recommend REALTORS® have a Desktop computer with a minimum of 64 Megabytes (MB) of RAM, 400 MegaHertz (MHz) of processor speed, 4 Gigabytes (GB) of hard drive, 56X CD-ROM drive, 3 ½ inch floppy drive, a mouse, a keyboard, and a pair of good speakers. In addition, if you are preparing flyers for open houses, you may want to invest money on a scanner and/or a digital camera. Scanners allow you to scan images from properties that you have previously taken photographs of. If you want to streamline the process, a digital camera is very beneficial. The picture can be taken instantly by a digital camera and converted to digital images. These digital images will then be uploaded to your computer for creating flyers, Web pages, and so on."

> *Professional Profile*
>
> Carol de Losada
> Carol@besthomesREALTOR.com
> Century 21 SCVA, Campbell, California
> Years in Business: 10
>
> **"You need to buy your tools before you go out and you need to know how to use them. Have a computer, a desktop and a laptop, if you can."**

A good number of REALTORS® are investing in laptops and for good reason. Lap top computers make traveling into the field and writing up offers more convenient, especially with the advent of electronic forms. Some REALTORS®, especially those newer to technology, seem to shy away from lap top computers. It is understandable that some people prefer the "big-ness" of a desktop computer, with the large screen and typewriter-like keyboard. There are, however, benefits associated with laptops, the main one being portability. You literally can take your laptop anywhere and plug it in, go on line, access all of your files, even pack along a portable printer for increased convenience. In addition, you can always have a large monitor and traditional keyboard at home to plug your laptop into when you're working from that location.

There are many REALTORS® who have both a laptop and a desktop and who simply update information from one system to the other. There are also a good deal of REALTORS® who use their office desktops when at the office and a laptop when out in the field, and of course, there are still those who own a desktop at home, use the office desktop at work, and carry a laptop in the field. The options are many and the choice is yours. The most important thing is to find what suits your style and budget and proceed accordingly.

Not everyone can break into the business and afford to go out and buy two new computer systems. Some will prefer a desktop, some will recognize the value of a laptop, and many will go for both-the choice is ultimately yours.

Professional Profile

Candy McGrath
Ncentiv@exis.net
Long & Foster,
Years in Business: 19

"It really helps to have a laptop for all entries and to make sure that you back up your records."

Along the lines of equipment we must also consider printers, digital cameras and, more recently, Palm Pilots, to name the most current. Printers are essential and should be purchased as part of the whole computer system. Ask the sales representative what kind of printer they suggest will best be supported by the computer you have selected. Printers come in many varieties. In order to print documents, the main criteria is that you have a basic color printer that can be procured easily for two to three hundred dollars, often even less.

Digital cameras are the new rage in real estate and for good cause. Instead of waiting and hoping for a good shot of your new listing, a digital camera will give you instant results. You'll know, right there on the spot, if the image you took is a good one, and if it isn't, you can simply take another-no film wasted. Perhaps even more beneficial is the "development" process of digital cameras. Actually, the development process is nothing more than plugging your camera into your computer and "downloading" the file (the picture(s)) onto your computer system. You can imagine how easy this makes it for you to print out picture-perfect flyers of your listings at greatly reduced costs. Moreover, as you will learn about when we discuss the Internet, digital pictures are ideal for promoting your properties on the web.

Palm Pilots promise to provide a powerful punch to the way you do business. The ability to check and send email from out on the road, offers many conveniences. Additionally, there are some software programs that allow you to incorporate the use of a Palm Pilot for more streamlined results.

If you are just starting out in the industry, a digital camera and Palm Pilot probably don't need to be the first things you rush out and buy. You'll definitely need a cell phone and computer and a printer though, not to mention access to copy and fax machines. There will be plenty of time for advanced technology (and money to invest into it) as you start closing transactions. For REALTORS® a bit more seasoned though, digital photography and Palm Pilot use are gifts from the heavens that seem to offer unlimited possibilities.

THE INTERNET

The buzzword of recent years has made its way into the real estate business in a big way. The World Wide Web is now an integral part of the real estate industry and will continue to be so even to the extent that your clients will be able, eventually, to buy a home from you without even meeting you. Electronic commerce is and will continue, to expand the possibilities as we know them. Keeping with the present though, let's consider some of the ways the Internet can impact your business today. While there are many new, more technologically advanced features popping up everyday, the initial and primary focus here will rest upon Internet advertising, email marketing, and using the web as your own resource tool.

Internet advertising actually covers quite a bit of territory. Here we will attempt to provide an overview of the main ground. For our purposes, Internet advertising is using the opportunity afforded by the Internet to advertise both your listings and yourself and certainly, with some creativity, you can already see the possibilities. Therefore, it is important to recognize, that here we are only noting the current most common forms of Internet advertising and that you should feel free to explore even more possibilities. Internet Advertising actually can be broken down a bit so that it does not seem to be so overwhelming to those who are still unsure of what an ISP account really is.

Professional Profile

Mary Funk
Mfunkrelo@aol.com
Realty Executives, Santa Clarita, California
Years in Business: 23

"My company has it's own magazine, website, and large market presence. It's important to be on at least one website."

WEBSITES

Internet advertising might be boiled down to one word…websites. As a REALTOR®, it would do you good to invest in obtaining your own website. The good news is that there are many, many opportunities for you to get free web-space to house your website. Moreover, there are many opportunities still to have someone help you with your website. You can either learn for yourself the not-so difficult task of keeping your site current with new listings, or pay someone else, so that you can pursue your real passion, selling properties.

A website is merely a place on the Internet where you can show images of your listings, along with detailed descriptions, prices, and anything else you want prospective homebuyers and sellers to know. Of course, you also want to take this opportunity to sell yourself. Many REALTORS® put their own photo on their website and ALL REALTORS® put their email address-which we will cover. Besides your very own, unique website, there are ample opportunities to expand.

More and more companies are recognizing the power of a well done website. If your company has its own website, and this might be a good broker-interview question, make sure your listings and your professional information is listed. Also, this is no time to be shy. If you have earned designations or won awards, make sure they're noted on your website. Company websites often get more traffic than personal websites, but that too, depends upon your marketing efforts and your listing information and desirability. Still, there are many other websites that would love to display your listings.

In addition to your own MLS service, many of which are posting local listings, there are websites that are happy to place your listings on line, either free or for a fee. Some of these sites are listed in Appendix A, but there are new ones surfacing all the time, so it's best to do your homework and ask around.

> *Professional Profile*
>
> Beth Ferester
>
> Ferester@ferester.com
>
> The Ferester Team at Coldwell Banker, Houston and the Woodlands, Texas
>
> Years in Business: 20
>
> **"The Internet is my marketing key. Last year, 25% of my business came from the Internet of which I only invested about 5% of my marketing dollars. The results speak for themselves."**

In order to understand why it is you should care about having all of your listings posted on the web, let us consider a few self-explanatory examples.

1) You live and work in Colorado. A nice couple from Kentucky is considering moving to Denver and need to find a home (and a REALTOR®). They start looking for properties and agents in Denver on line…will they see you and your listings?

2) Another nice couple is driving around the neighborhood they wish to buy in and see your "For Sale Sign." Being the tech-savvy people they are, they go home and check your company website to find out more about the property…will it be there? Will you?

3) A seller is deciding which agent to list with so he goes on line to find out the area expert who he knows will take advantage of technology-focused marketing.

4) A buyer's agent in town is looking for listings to show his client. The REALTOR® is fairly up to speed on technology and prefers working with other REALTORS® who are the same. He recognizes the

convenience of email communications. Will he be showing your listings to his buyer?

Here is where digital photography can truly pay off. Once you've taken an image of your listings, they can be conveniently "posted" on your website. This is merely a matter of "uploading" the picture file onto your website and detailed instructions are easily accessible from online searches, books, and might even be included with your digital camera instructions.

These are just a few simple examples, but the list is endless. We live in an era of technology. Buyers and sellers have computers, send emails, and surf the web. When it's time to buy or list a home, many of them are going on line. This is especially true for those looking in locations further away, such as out of state or out of town. Having a web presence in this day and age is almost paramount and any REALTOR® who fails to take advantage of all the "free" forms of Internet advertising will inevitably pay the cost.

Professional Profile

Margaret Bannochie
Margaret@tulsa-home.com
RE/MAX Executives, Tulsa, Oklahoma
Years in Business: 17

"Face to face contact is still really helpful. I use to send out a lot of mailings, however, I now focus more specifically on my sphere of influence. I have a good web page and do a lot of Internet marketing…it works!"

EMAIL & ISP

In order to get on line or create and build a site, you'll need to have on line access, or an ISP (Internet Service Provider) and email software. Both of these offer unlimited choices. Because the competition is stiff between the various ISP's available today, most will provide you with free web space to create your own web page and offer instruction and assistance to get it built. There are also many opportunities for free email addresses. The best solution is to ask other REALTORS® and people you know with technical savvy, which providers they use. While you can always switch, remember the inconvenience of changing website URL and email addresses is not unlike changing your phone number; you'll need to change your business cards and call everyone you know to implement the change effectively. Therefore, if you do your homework and ask around, you are much more likely to find service providers who will meet your needs and satisfy your on line adventures.

Professional Profile

Tamara Ross
Tross1214@aol.com
RE/MAX First,
Years in Business: 15

"One of the most effective things I use the Internet for is to market other agents in my area, as well as the general public."

EMAIL MARKETING

Electronic mail is a very big and important part of all this Internet advertising business. Advertising on the Internet can only be successful if the prospective client or other REALTOR® has immediate access to contact you. Although it's nothing to laugh about, there have actually been great agent websites, complimented by beautiful property images, mission statements and additional information, all followed up with a telephone number and a mailing address. Understand immediately that the appeal of instant action is what makes the web what it is. When people go online, they want to click buttons and get results. They don't want to grab a piece of paper and jot down a telephone number and go to the phone (maybe having to get off line to get a dial tone….) and place a call-especially if it's long distance. People want immediate results and instant responses and that can only happen if you have an email address. In addition to allowing others to contact you immediately, email is an outstanding source of marketing.

Professional Profile

Andrew Peck
Apeck@royalpacific.com
Royal Pacific Realty Group, Vancouver, British Columbia
Years in Business: 14

"Email to a regular group of clients on a twice monthly basis. Also, in my humble opinion, the Internet is a research tool…people will not make a purchase decision from a picture on their monitor, however, they will use it to do their homework."

Not only is email an outstandingly easy way to keep in constant contact with your clients, affiliates, and other agents, but it also provides you with instant documentation of what was said and to whom. Email doesn't need to take away the personal touch of customer service that so many REAL-TORS® recognize as vital, but it certainly can add expediency to nearly any transaction. Email marketing however, is a good communication platform for both existing and potential clients alike.

Consider the convenience of sending all of your past and potential clients an email newsletter. Email marketing is an excellent means of generating new business and keeping in contact with previous clientele. Companies who specialize in creating email lists, based on your specific criteria, area, income level, homeowner, etc., can be easily found with online searches. An important caveat to keep in mind whenever you are "cold-calling" via email is that you must always include an easy way for the recipients to let you know if they do not wish to receive any more emails from you. This is generally referred to in email marketing as the "unsubscribe option." If someone asks to be removed from your email-marketing list, then by all means, remove their name and do not send them any more emails.

Professional Profile

Richard Walsh
Walsh@flinthills.com
Blanton Realty
Years in Business: 25

"Today, an agent needs to find the biggest bang for the communication buck, Internet ads and good referrals. There are always saturation techniques through traditional mailings, but the Internet is the way to go."

In addition to marketing potential clients, think about emailing REALTORS® who sell in your listing neighborhood, to help you move your inventory.

When you begin to imagine all of the effective ways email marketing can streamline your communication efforts, for much less money than traditional paper-based marketing, you'll be eager to have the whole world on line!

Professional Profile

Don King
Donking-homes.com
RE/MAX Rancho Bernardo, San Diego, California
Years in Business: 11

"Ask everyone for their email address—it's much faster to market by email than conventional mail and it's free!"

SOFTWARE

Beyond the general operating system software and the various software you will need to work your printers, scanners, internal faxes, and so on, you will also want to have a few software programs that help to make you as effective and productive as possible. There are at least four kinds of programs that many REALTORS® agree you'll need to be your most efficient. A good contact management program, word processing, electronic forms, and desktop publishing. Of course, there are literally dozens of other software programs out there that certainly are worthy of your time and consideration, but it might be best to first address and understand the basics, prior to breaking new ground.

Professional Profile

Karen Allen
KarenAllen@bellsouth.net
Coldwell Banker, Fulton Realty, Peachtree City, Georgia
Years in Business: 10

"New REALTORS® should own computer programs that help keep them organized."

There are literally dozens of contact management programs available. A contact management program is simply a software program that holds your client information in some kind of database, and allows you an easy avenue for keeping in contact, marketing, and following up with your client database. This however, is only the basic premise of such programs. An unlimited number of REALTORS® from all over the country attested to using one particular contact management software more than any other, Top Producer. Top Producer software spans well beyond traditional contact management software in that it is specifically designed to make the committed REALTOR® a "top producer," Check Appendix A to learn more about the features this software provides as well as contact information for the dealer nearest to you. Contact management is essential to your success in real estate sales. Another important step in e-commerce is electronic forms.

The contracts you write are subject to everyone else being able to read your handwriting. They also can take a significant amount of time to fill out. Imagine the convenience of having your contracts on your computer and filling out a few things on just one form and then having all of that information automatically transfer itself on all the other forms you will be using for the entire transaction! Any REALTOR® who has filled out a seemingly endless pile of paper, will immediately recognize what a savior this kind of software can be. WINFORMS®2000 and ZIPFORMS® are electronic forms software that accomplishes this task with ease and also allows you to email your contracts to clients, other agents, and even service providers. Again, see Appendix A for more information. The additional two software programs you'll need to master might even be bundled in your operating system.

For the most part, all new systems come with some kind of word processing program. A word-processing program is simply a software program that allows you to write letters and create a basic flyer. The more advanced the program, the wider array of features usually included. If you have acquired a decent word-processing program, you might find that you don't need a desktop publishing program. If you have invested in an office suite of some kind (a software package that contains several of the more popular programs), there might even be a desktop publishing program included. A good word processing program is essential to write letters, produce basic flyers, and document important information.

This list is by no means exhaustive of the multitude of tasks that can be accomplished with adequate software programs. It is not unreasonable to plan your schedule (including your immediate and long-term goals), manage your finances, and database your contacts, all from the convenience and comfort of your priceless piece of equipment-your computer.

Professional Profile
Terry Hunter, CEO surfmls@earthlink.net
Firm: Hunter Pacific, Irvine, California

Years in Business: 20

"Several years ago, before WINForms®2000 software, my wife and I made several hundred thousand dollars in land sale commissions, primarily because we were able to present 300 flawlessly correct offers in a 90 day period. Back then, I had to create a computerized offer generator myself, because electronic contracts were non-existent. Wow! If only I'd had the extra power of WINForms®2000 then.... But I have it NOW and I'm KEEPING it forever!"

TECHNOLOGY SUMMARY

In conclusion of our technology talk, understand that there is no conclusion. Technology is a constantly growing, always evolving, permanent component of our business world. And, moreover, an integral part of the real estate industry.

Today, consumers have access to an abundance of information that is as close as a click of their mouse. In order to serve them effectively and to keep on top of the competition, it will be critical for you to dive into the world of technology, full speed ahead!

Professional Profile

Joel Goodness
Firm: Coldwell Banker, Beverly Hills, California

"In the time I've been working in real estate, there have been many new and exciting technical advances in the field. We are the new breed of agents and with that comes another saying…'Knowledge is Power!' The more you know, the more you can pull from in any situation. We are now an Internet world…and we all must embrace it! The Multiple Listing Service is on the Internet, making the search easy for those who know and understand this new technology. We have access to acquire our own websites and make them work for us in addition to the cell phone, Palm pilot, Virtual tours, and digital cameras. Escrow companies, title companies and several other affiliated companies are jumping aboard the Internet highway and making our job that much efficient, so in turn, we can give back to our clients and make the real estate experience that much less stressful and more streamlined."

Equipment Record

Item	Serial Number	Date	Tech Support Contact Info

_____
_____
_____
_____

Software Record

Name   Serial# Password   Date   Tech Support Contact Info

_____
_____
_____
_____
_____
_____
_____
_____
_____
_____

ISPN & Email

Provider   Password   Login   Email Address/URL

_____
_____
_____
_____
_____
_____

Tech Support:_____

MONEY MATTERS

*"Finance is the art of passing currency from hand to hand
until it finally disappears."*
Robert W. Sarnoff

Professional Profile

S.W. Ellis
Sellis@unr.net
Blue Bird Homes & Lands, Inc., Monticello, FL
Years in Business: 11

**"You may spend thousands of dollars in this business before you
make a cent."**

It makes the world go around. It makes us smile when we have loads of it
and mad as the dickens when we don't have enough. Money is a particularly important incentive for many REALTORS® because if transactions
don't close, bills don't get paid. This, however, is not intended to talk
about earning potential or specific dollar amounts, but instead saving,
planning, and paying those much-dreaded taxes.

Professional Profile

Lee Bowman
Lee@leebowman.com
RE/MAX Lake Front Realty, Smith Mountain Lake, Virginia
Years in Business: 15

"Create a tax savings account and put 12-15% of every check you make into that account. Mark your calendar well in advance to indicate the four months per year when you must submit your estimated taxes to both federal and state."

While it certainly makes sense to advise anybody in any kind of business to save money, in this industry it holds vital importance. The flip side to unlimited earning potential in the real estate industry is the tax crunch. Yes, as your own boss, so to speak, you are responsible for paying your own taxes. What that means, is that the big commission check issued by your broker has not had any taxes deducted. No, that doesn't mean it's tax free income!

Many new REALTORS®, and even a few established ones, have had to learn this lesson the hard way. You have to pay taxes. The final twist to this dilemma is that you are in the midst of an industry with a market that's not always so easy to predict. The only intelligent way then, to protect yourself and your financial interests, is to sock away a percentage of each commission check in an account that can be earning interest until it's time to go to Uncle Sam.

Professional Profile

Dave Olson
Doltd@srv.net
Century 21 Greater Land Co., Idaho Falls, Idaho
Years in Business: 6

"Set yourself up on a budget and live within it. For example, 25% for taxes, 25% for savings, and the balance for paying yourself and bills."

Professional Profile

Mary Conover
Mary@loudounRealEstate.com
RE/MAX Renaissance, Leesburg, Virginia
Years in Business: 10

"It's so easy to spend the thousands that you earn, but if you do, you'll pay for it later. For EVERY deal, take 30% off the top and put it in a totally separate account for the IRS. Make quarterly payments. I learned this the hard way! As soon as you have a couple of good deals under your belt, and several more lined up, set up a Limited Liability Company and pay yourself from it. You'll need to work with a CPA who knows the business. Plan to be strict with yourself the first two to three years and it will pay off in the long run."

There are literally so many tax laws and implications that you need to beware of, that it really is essential you establish a relationship with a reputable tax accountant. For your added benefit, an excellent book on taxes entitled *Tax Planning Strategies for the Self-Employed*, written by A.J. Cataldo, can provide you with valuable insight into the tax arena that you may have not even considered. Cataldo's articles have appeared in many real estate publications and here, with the author's permission, are informative articles that would behoove you to read.

Professional Profile

Angela M. Paulauskas

Ampaulauskas@@Juno.com

Watson Realty Corporation

Years in Business: 2

"Besides saving money to pay taxes, save EVERY receipt and keep perfect documentation of all your expenses!"

Deducting the Home Office
by A.J. Cataldo, Ph.D., CPA, CMA

as adapted from Chapter 11 of Tax Planning Strategies for the Self-Employed published by Publish America, Inc.

Much mysticism surrounds the home-office deduction. Frequently, tax accountants advise their clients against legitimately deducting their home office. Consider the following: The depreciation of the business use portion of your home office is otherwise not deductible. Therefore, a mere $1,000 deduction for depreciation would save the taxpayer $433 (assumes a 28 percent federal income tax bracket plus the 15.3 percent self-employment tax equals a total of 43.3 percent multiplied by $1,000 equals $433; state income tax savings have not been included in this computation) per year, every year!

Even if you sell the house, the recapture (the reason many tax accountants give to their clients for not wanting to take this deduction) of any depreciation results in a permanent tax savings of the self-employment tax of 15.3 percent! The business use portion of otherwise non-deductible utilities, repairs, homeowner's association dues, basic cable, etc., result in permanent income and self-employment tax savings. For example, again using $1,000, an additional permanent tax savings of $433 results.

For taxpayers otherwise unable to itemize, the business use portion of real estate taxes and home mortgage interest become deductible! Again, using the $1,000 example, an additional permanent tax savings of $433. For taxpayers otherwise able to itemize, the shifting of the business use portion of real estate taxes and home mortgage interest saves an additional 15.3 percent for the self-employment tax. Again, using the $1,000 example, this means an additional permanent tax savings of $153. Limitations and other strategic considerations apply, so be sure to discuss this topic with your tax accountant!

Keeping Interest Expense 100% Deductible

by A.J. Cataldo, Ph.D., CPA, CMA as adapted from Chapter 10 of Tax Planning Strategies for the Self-Employed published by Publish America, Inc.

There are 5 categories of interest expense, as follows: (1) business interest, (2) passive activity interest, (3) qualified residence interest, (4) investment interest, and (5) personal interest.

For the self-employed taxpayer, business interest classification provides the greatest tax benefit. For example, business interest expense of $1,000, for a self-employed taxpayer in the 28 percent federal income tax bracket (and ignoring state income tax-related savings) would provide tax savings of $433 (28 percent plus 15.3 percent equals 43.3 percent multiplied by $1,000 equals $433).

Compare this to qualified residence interest expense, where the self-employment tax savings are not achieved, and the tax savings are only $280 on this same $1,000 (28 percent multiplied by $1,000 equals $280).

Passive activity interest and investment interest expense may result in the same tax savings as qualified residence interest, but may be subject to more stringent limitations. Personal interest expense is simply not deductible.

Therefore, the simple rule is to BORROW FOR BUSINESS PUR-POSES FIRST!

There are some pitfalls to be avoided. Tracing rules should be considered and some limitations and other strategic considerations may apply, so be sure to discuss this topic with your tax accountant!

WHEN THE WELL RUNS DRY

We like to think we'll always have all the money we'll ever need, however, that's not always the case. The real estate industry can be sporadic at times; either very busy or very slow. Generally speaking, if you plan well and save the same, you can squeak through the lean times.

Professional Profile

Professional Profile

Jan Hettick
Jhettick@earthlink.net
Palos Verdes Realty, Palos Verdes Estates, California
Years in Business: 40

"Plan your money and your cash flow six months in advance. Have plenty of credit available for the lean periods. When you close an escrow, PAY OFF as much as possible- invest in yourself."

Generally speaking, a number of REALTORS® acknowledged getting through the dry spells by relying on credit, a second source of income, or borrowing. The catch here is to make sure you replace whatever you took. If you find you need to take $500 out on a credit card one month, when you close an escrow the next month, pay that $500 back. This is the most effective way to keep from feeling the crunch of inflated interest rates that usually accompanies those little plastic cards.

Because money is such an important issue, and such a slippery one at that, it is important that you take good care of the money you earn. Taking good care of it means that you invest wisely. In her book, *The 9 Steps To Financial Freedom*, Suze Orman tells us there are only three ways in this world to get money. First you can earn it from hard work, second you can inherit it, and third, you can invest it wisely, which happens to be Ms. Orman's personal favorite.

"It is not respectful to yourself, to others, or to your money not to take full advantage of the 401(k)s or IRAs or other retirement plans that are available to you. It is not respectful to yourself, to others or to your money not to face your debts, to learn the basics of investing, and to guard over your money, making sure that every penny you're spending is a penny that must be spent. What day you pay your bills, when you send in your taxes, and what hidden costs you pay from your checking account all can make a difference in how much money gets attracted your way."

Ms. Orman's advice is smart, and it would be wise for any agent, new or established, to read this and other books on smart investing, as well as speaking in detail to a well-reputed real estate accountant on how you can best make your money work for you. Remember, when you're racking up the commission checks, it's great if you've accounted for your taxes and put that money aside, but in order to stay ahead in this game called life, you will also need to consider retirement. Your broker has no profit sharing plan for you and you've got no one besides yourself socking money into a pension plan. Invest and spend intelligently, planning for your future all the while.

The following pages provides you with a proto type of the kind record keeping that will assist you in tracking your income and keeping track of what set aside for taxes. In addition to this careful planning, it will be critical that you keep track of all your monthly expenses, from supplies, marketing, mileage, to business lunches, and the myriad of other little expense that often creep us in the course of a year. Document, document, document. Save receipts, note dates, and even property addresses when applicable. You can never keep too many records when it comes to your income and expenses.

Finally, beyond a tax accountant, you may want to consider the possibility of working with a professional investment broker. Some financial institutes offer stock investment assistance as an added member benefit. It is essential that you explore now, while you are still working, what kind of retirement options you have before you. There are numerous agents still selling real estate well into their seventies, so it's not as if there is a forced age of retirement. As a matter of fact, working at something you love has actually been proven to keep you alive and healthy longer than if you retire and sit around all day. Nevertheless, be smart when it comes to your future, especially where your money is concerned.

SMART MONEY TIPS
- Set aside money from every commission check for quarterly taxes
- Only use credit as a last resort and then repay it promptly
- Keep track of all of your closed transaction and how much you made
- Keep track of every single work related expense, no matter how small
- Work with a reputable tax accountant and find out all you can on how to make your money work better for you
- Save as much as you can to get you through the dry spells
- Find a good financial investor or advisor who can help you plan for a comfortable retirement

Financial Planning

Accountant Name and Contact Information:

_____

_____

_____

Financial Institute & Information:

_____

_____

_____

Record of Properties sold for the year_____
Property Address Closed Date Commission Earned Amount Reserved

_____

_____

_____

_____

_____

_____

_____

_____

_____

_____

_____

_____

_____

_____

_____

_____

_____

_____

_____

_____

_____

Deductions (keep track of your mileage separately) Year:_____
     Date   Purpose / Kind of Expense   Cost   Paid To

_____

_____

_____

_____

_____

_____

_____

_____

_____

_____

_____

_____

_____

_____

_____

_____

_____

_____

_____

_____

_____

MOTIVATED FOR SUCCESS

"Genius is one percent inspiration and ninety-nine percent perspiration."
Thomas Edison

REALTORS® are salespeople and salespeople like to be motivated. We like to be inspired, convinced, driven, and ignited. It's in our nature to take our enthusiasm and share it with our clients, families, and co-workers. You will find that there are certain "masters" in the real estate industry, ready to cheer you on to a better, faster, more profitable system. It is not within the scope of this book to evaluate the many different seminars out there, real estate specific or otherwise. However, many top producers have reported that they find motivational seminars very effective in taking them to the next level. While there are very knowledgeable speakers out there who have valid advice and enthusiasm to share, it is important to keep things in their proper perspective.

Professional Profile

Bonnie Casper

Bcasper@lomey.com

Comey & Sheperd, Cincinnati, Ohio

Years in Business: 15

"Everything you do or fail to do leads to your reputation and success. You are the president of you!"

Motivation is vital to success in the real estate business and many an agent praises the work of well-known real estate masters. Whether it's attending a seminar, listening to audio tapes in the car, or reading inspirational words of selling gurus, keeping yourself in the right state of mind is crucial. Also, remember that many of these kinds of expenditures, might qualify as tax-deductions, so talk to your accountant.

Technology has provided but another useful and convenient way in which to keep you professionally moved and motivated; the Internet.

Here is an article reprinted with permission of the author, Philip Humbert. This serves as an excellent motivational resource for any salesperson, and contains the basic premise that can literally be applied to all facets of your real-estate-selling life:

The Seven Sisters of Success
By Philip Humbert

I recently had a chance to interview several groups of extremely successful people. A handful are famous athletes, several are nationally known artists, writers or politicians, and all are multi-millionaires. I asked them for the keys, or essential factors that allowed them to accomplish so much more than the rest of us.

Their answers included a wide variety of specifics, but to an astonishing degree, 7 items came up in every discussion. I've called them the "Seven Sisters of Success", and want to share them with you.

1.   **Self-awareness.**
The first thing that struck me about these men and women was the degree to which they understood themselves. They know their values and goals, and are comfortable with the choices they have made in life. They admitted some regrets and mistakes, but they have made peace with the past and are eager, confident and optimistic about the future.

2.   **Specific Goals.**
Every single one of these 26 people has written goals, ranging from 30-day projects to 10-year programs. I was impressed that their goals are IN WRITING. Athletes had performance targets, and the business leaders had sales goals. They all had family or personal goals that were just as detailed as their professional objectives. The advice we have all heard about writing down your goals really works!

3.   **Powerful Networks.**
They all acknowledged their network of friends and colleagues. Each one gave credit to a mentor or friend who taught them the ropes, opened doors, or gave them a chance when they needed it. They were profoundly grateful and appreciated that success is the result of partnering with many people over many years.

4.   **Surprising Idealism.**

I was surprised at the degree to which these seasoned, mature individuals openly discussed their ideals. Some talked about religious beliefs, others framed it in political or psychological terms, but they all want to make a difference, fulfill a life-purpose, or pursue a dream. They are motivated by a desire to create a better world, to contribute, and to help others.

5.   **Intense Pragmatism.**

Balanced with their idealism, these highly successful people were extremely practical. They are solution-focused, and use technology, information, and skills to reach their most important goals. They were not interested in theories, or in defending past choices or old traditions. They use practical tools to help them reach their goals.

6.   **Extraordinary Curiosity.**

They observe culture, read the paper, read about their industry, and try to learn about everything around them. They read about politics and religion; they want to know about the stock market and cooking. I was surprised that most of them were not "experts" in the usual sense, but they are extremely educated, bright and curious. They have earned their doctorates in "real life". Very interesting!

7.   **Personal Discipline.**

They don't waste time, and they don't lie to themselves. They don't exaggerate or minimize, and they don't generalize. These people were precise when they spoke about their age, relationships, business affairs or dreams. Numbers and dates, dollars and cents were important to them, and I found them easy to talk with, and very clear in their communications.

What impressed me was that the keys to their success were not related to family or background. They had not been born wealthy, and only about half completed college. They did not seem "driven" for success. They did not make their fortunes in high-tech or by winning a lottery. Instead, they followed a plan that created persistent, high levels of success or a lifetime.

Each of these skills can be learned by anyone! There are no "secrets" of success, and talent, family and luck had little to do with it. These highly successful people knew what they wanted, and used their networks, hard work, patience and discipline to achieve outstanding results. So can you!

Copyright © 2000 by Philip E. Humbert, PhD. Email: Coach@philiphumbert.com Website: http://www.philiphumbert.com. Visit Dr Humbert's website for over 250 pages of articles, Top 10 lists, humor, quotes, tips and tools for your success! There's a free book on making (and keeping!) more money, and a FREE motivational newsletter. Check it out at: http://www.philiphumbert.com

To find even more motivational tips, visit your bookstore in person or online and look for "Motivation." Look under "Sales," "Inspiration," and "Communication" too for your key word searches. In addition, there are plenty of web resources, like the one noted above, that publish positive and proficient motivational strategies that can help to keep you mentally on top of your game. Some of these sites will even email you a daily motivational thought!

The appendix lists a series of effective publications that have been written for the real estate professional-many of these double as a means of motivation, however, when searching out motivational material, it is not necessary to limit yourself to one specific industry-motivation can be derived and thereby applied, to any business.

Interview With the President

Richard A. Mendenhall, CIPS, CRB, GRI

RE/MAX Boone Realty, Columbia Missouri- Owner/120+ REALTORS

Years in Business: 27

President 2001 National Association of REALTORS®

President Mendenhall is an energetic and enthusiastic person who openly shares his strong values and deep-rooted respect for all of human life by sharing some of the following sayings and quotes that he has heard along the way. Richard acknowledges that inspiration can be found nearly anywhere. Reading books, famous speeches, attending seminars, and searching the Internet can all result in motivational tidbits that stay on your mind and inspire you to succeed. Here are some thoughts that keep our NAR President in his favorite frame of mind:

"Ready, Aim, Fire"

"Success in real estate is a four-letter word- G U T S."

"No one got up the courage to storm Bastille after receiving a memo."

"The quickest way to acquire self-confidence is to do exactly what you are afraid to do."

"You should not confuse your career with your life."

Henry Ford was noted as saying that "Whether you think you will succeed or think you will fail, you are right." The meaning behind this is quite simply to hold in your mind the positive, see the good, and go for the gusto. This is an industry filled with opportunity, but it can also present challenges that may, at times, seem insurmountable. The most important thing is to keep and maintain a positive outlook which focuses toward your listing and sales success and never considers the possibility of failure.

THE JOURNEY JUST BEGINS

Looking back, we started with the initial steps of becoming a licensed REALTOR®, finding a broker, dealing with time, money, clients, and technology. Now you're ready to take action; ready to create or continue a career that holds more promise than perhaps any other. You're ready to excel, make money, and rise to the top.

Even if you are already licensed to sell real estate, by following the guidelines laid out for you here, you stand to increase the success and productivity of your business.

Recognize that becoming a part of organized real estate is the true premise to a rewarding real estate career. By joining and supporting your local, state, and national associations, you have created a calling card that lends distinction to the industry. Not only will you find the experience gratifying and rewarding, but you will also enjoy the opportunity of sharing with your clients and potential clients that you have joined the upper ranks of those held to the highest standard of professionalism and ethics. Become involved in your community, take an interest in your farm area, take an interest in issues and laws that may affect your business.

Part of being a professional is keeping abreast of current trends, laws, and local policies that will impact your business. Whether it's a new listing contract or a city sewer law, if it affects your business or your clients, you need to know about it. Generally speaking, continuing educational opportunities abound in the real estate industry. Whether you choose exciting live lectures, correspondence courses, or the newest and most time and cost effective means, on-line education, stay smart and learn as much as possible. Remember that the competition is high and that being armed with knowledge is the best kind of ammunition available. Continuing education, trade publications, MLS meetings, and your weekly office meetings will all serve as valuable attributes on your way to the top.

Regardless of everything else you do, in order to find true success, you'll need to manage your time. Effective time management techniques, such as those we discussed earlier, are crucial to top producing activity. There are too many tasks in the busy REALTOR'S® life to not write them down. Even dropping off an offer or meeting an appraiser qualifies as an entry in your calendar. Furthermore, the majority of agents interviewed noted that they make it a special point to record personal and family time as appointments and hold them as such. This is a fast-paced and exciting industry to be sure, but if you are not in control of your calendar, it will surely control you. For the most productive measures, keep your daily schedule closely aligned with your goals.

Writing down your goals will inevitably be the most effective means of reaching them. Endless studies have identified that there is true validity in goal setting. Moreover, it is thought that by putting your goals on paper, you somehow breathe life into them. Whether it's a matter of making us more accountable or simply some secret success technique, does not matter. What does matter is that you have a plan, both short and long term, that you put down on paper and revisit often to chart your progress. You will be amazed at your success.

Remember that everyone you meet is a potential client. It's important then to always maintain a presentable image and respectful attitude because you never know when you'll meet your next buyer or seller. It could be in line at the bank or in conversation at your child's school, so be prepared. Part of being prepared and marketing yourself includes always having business cards in your pocket or your purse and "marking" yourself as a REALTOR®. Whether you have a specially engraved license plate, a firm or REALTOR® polo shirt, or an "I Love Referrals" tie tack, the point is that any way you can let the world know that you are in business to list and sell houses, the better off you are. Items and apparel that advertise your business, help to promote your business. So whether someone strikes up a conversation in the grocery store parking lot, wondering exactly what kind of referrals your license plate frame is asking them to provide, or you pick up a buyer who isn't clear on what the little "R" in REALTOR® stands for, you've brought attention to yourself and that's what we call self-promotion.

You will of course, need to consider some overall marketing strategies. These strategies will be directly commensurate with the kind of budget you are working with. Many REALTORS® start out with very small marketing budgets and that shouldn't discourage you in the least. There is something rewarding about building your business from the ground up. Even if it mean sticking address labels on 250 postcards while you and your family are watching television. In addition to direct mail, don't ever underestimate the power of personal touch. Many a top producer proclaimed their ascent toward success started out with a steady step in the neighborhood. Whether you walk your farm area, door to door, call on the telephone, or make it a point to get involved in community events, getting your name, your face, and your intentions out there is really the underlying premise to marketing yourself successfully. This also means that any kind of ad space you can afford, professional pieces you can have printed up, or flyer distribution service you can use, are all worthwhile investments. It's always a good idea to talk with other agents about self-promotion to find out what works and what doesn't. Keep in mind though, that what works for you, might not be right for someone else. Marketing is one area where creativity and innovation are highly revered. Be different.

Take the time you need when selecting a broker. Make sure the fit is right and the office environment is one that you find supportive and motivating. Remember the importance of cultivating an honest and open line of communication with your broker. Ask other agents in the office how they like working there and then pay close attention to how you think you'd like working with them.

Remember too, that brokers can afford to be just as selective. Each agent they hire uses desk space, telephones, and other miscellaneous expenses out of their allocated budget. This means that most brokers are looking for the cream of the crop. Of course, this doesn't mean that a good many brokers aren't willing to hire a new agent, as long as that new agent shows potential. Honesty, ethics, and enthusiasm with a capital "E" are the most important qualities you can promote to potential brokers who you'd like to work with. Also, once your license is hung, an active and aggressive marketing strategy, coupled with committed customer follow up, will not only make your broker sigh with joy, but it will keep those commission checks coming your way!

Commission checks and customer follow up are directly related to your communications skills. In the section on communications, we spent a fair amount of time revealing some of the more common objections you will come across with buyers and sellers. It is correct to state that the variety of situations and the diverse ways of handling them will be as unique as you are. The situations we presented do, however, happen to be the most common chief objections that REALTORS® tend to mention.

How you handle these, or any other obstacles or conflicts, is completely up to you. It will be essential that you always act within the high standards you have committed to, and to defer to your broker for input and direction, especially when you are newer to the business or there is a potential problem.

The general communications scenarios that have been provided can take you a long way toward improved client relationships. Listening, repeating, and above all, understanding the buyer or seller from their point of view, are all key to effectively communicating your point of view and overcoming their objections. Basic communication skills, regardless of your personal style, will undoubtedly have a positive impact on all areas of your personal and professional life.

In addition to client communications, you will be actively engaged with other industry professionals. Whether it is another agent, an escrow officer, or the pest control man, effective communication skills will be key to your success. Read the middle section over, at least one more time, to ensure that you have indeed acquired an unwavering grasp on the essentials of communicating effectively. Even the most seasoned of agents has become frustrated during heated conversations and lost sellers or buyers. This doesn't need to happen. By applying effective communications skills as part of your on-going qualities, you will rise far above those who fail to do so. Adopt communication techniques that work for you. Learn to overcome objectives in a manner that demonstrates to your clients that you listen and you care. This is the mark of a true professional.

Recognize affiliates as being on your side. Yes, they solicit you that same way you sometimes need to solicit potential clients, but they are indeed assets. Cultivating relationships built on trust and professional respect can be your saving grace in an industry that often spins faster than the speed of sound. Lenders and title companies are two of the most common vendors you will want to become familiar with, however there are many others who can contribute to the good of your business. Take time to listen and allow these affiliates opportunities to help you become a more efficient and effective REALTOR® with some of the outstanding assistance they are often willing to provide.

Technology is one area you might find yourself in need of assistance. To the novice and the skilled alike, the electronic age is mind-boggling. Between hardware, software, modems, cell phones, faxes, palm pilots, and so on, it's no wonder we sometimes shake our heads in defeat. The good news is that computers have progressively become easier to operate and the Internet, more easy to navigate. Literally anyone who can read, can follow the simple instructions for installing software and even setting up a web page, really! It's a good idea to take advantage of computer and software training whenever you have the chance. Whether through your REALTOR® association, or a private/public school, or even a book, keep yourself up to date in this rapidly changing arena. The real estate business is sure to evolve in technology. Your best bet is to invest in that laptop and electronic forms software just as soon as possible. Get your feet wet now, so when you're recording closings online next year, you'll be ready for it.

In addition, recognize the technology move as a blessing for real estate sales. Besides pagers and cell phones and faxes that enable far more effective modes of communication than available before, there is a menagerie of advertising potential. Internet marketing, email lists, web websites, and virtual tours are but the tip of the promotional iceberg that technology has introduced. More will surely surface.

It is vital to keep current and involved in the on-going opportunity that technology affords your business.

Technology will enhance your productivity, but money will manage it. We stated earlier that this can be a feast or famine business, but for the REALTOR® who is prepared, there should always be an entrée. Too many agents to mention have admitted the faux pas of learning the money management ropes the hard way. It is inevitable that when those commission checks start rolling in, you'll want to buy cars and houses and cruises to the Caribbean.

The beauty of this business is also the curse. You have to pay your own taxes. For those who are less experienced and tend to spend it when they get it, there comes a big shock at tax time when Uncle Sam comes calling. The beauty however, lies in the fact that when you sock away money each commission check, it's *you* who is collecting interest, not the government. Make that money work for you by keeping it safely reserved in a high-interest account of some kind, but most importantly, don't touch it!

Besides your tax responsibilities, remember to save for a rainy day. Even the most astute and aggressive real estate marketer has seen his share of showers. While building the basis of repeat and referral business will be your best defense against stormy weather, there might be times when no one is buying or selling real estate. Generally speaking, if and when these dry spells strike, you'll need to have a nest egg to see you through to the next transaction.

Avoid using credit cards unless it's absolutely essential-they can take longer to pay off then a mortgage and are much less rewarding.

The articles shared with you in the money management section were provided by a well-known and respected real estate tax professional. You should always affiliate yourself with an accountant and attorney well versed in the real estate industry.

The business basics are more concrete in understanding and application. Why then, is motivation so critical to success? For whatever the reason, one cannot deny the requirement for drive and enthusiasm to make it big in the real estate business. Whether you are sure and steady, or bouncing off the walls with energy, your enthusiasm is paramount to your success.

Your clients can tell if you enjoy your job. If you love your business, you will listen intently to their concerns, respond sincerely to their inquiries, and put genuine energy and effort into the relationship and the goal of finding or selling the property.

If you love your work it shows, if you don't, that shows too! Real estate sales require professionals committed to the success of their personal business as well as their industry. It isn't always easy to stay ahead of the competition when you feel like you're losing ground.

Most top producers are the first to admit that they get frustrated and have down days just as much as anybody else. The difference is that they rise above it. Top producers in real estate, as well as in life in general, choose to find the positive and the potential in each and every circumstance. The good is just as easy to spot as the bad, and pinpointing the potential takes you much further toward success.

Keep yourself motivated in whatever way works. Many agents attend inspirational seminars, read great books, listen to audio programs, and surround themselves with positive people. Affirming what is good in your life and focusing on the positive are two essential factors towards increased productivity. *Assuming* that you will succeed, plants the seed of expectation in your mind. Once that seed is planted, watered, and cared for, it is sure to flourish.

This is a business that knows no limit. You can make of yourself whatever you desire and take yourself to any level you please. It is all about commitment, effort, action, attitude, and common sense. By following the advice and applying the techniques presented to you here, you will undoubtedly rise to the top of your game.

Good Luck!

ABOUT THE AUTHOR

Tamara Dorris has been in the real estate industry for more than twelve years. Raised by a mother who is a REALTOR®, she became astutely aware of the many exciting, yet challenging, facets of the real estate industry. Her own experience has included being a REALTOR®, a title representative, selling real estate ad space, and several years working in marketing and communications at the largest state real estate trade association.

Tamara earned her Bachelor's Degree in psychology from Chapman University and her Master's Degree in Communications from Regis University. She is committed to the continuous study of communications, marketing, and self-empowerment, and has authored additional books to that end. She lives in Carmichael California with her family of six.

Note: The views in this book are not necessarily supported or endorsed by any local, state, or national real estate trade association, including the author's employer

Appendix A

TOOLS OF THE TRADE

While your skills, commitment, and energy are the main criteria for entering the real estate arena; there are other items that most REALTORS® deem necessary. This of course is in addition to those tools of technology, such as computers, cell phones, and copy machines that we have already discussed. There are many resources for various tools you will need and obviously you'll need to factor in cost and convenience as your guiding post. There are, however, a couple of points worthy of mention.

When you purchase your tools and supplies from your local association of REALTORS®, you are helping to support organized real estate with non-dues revenue. Your local association works hard to help you stay effective, trained, and knowledgeable about the industry. Not all local associations have room for a supply center, although many do. With the advent of technology, many local associations are now able to order your tools through online resources that are now available and profitable to them. If you can't find the products you are looking for from your local association, ask them if they have considered a website of their own, and if they have one, why not link it up to an outstanding supply resource, such as some of the ones noted here, so that you are able to help them generate more local revenues.

TOOLS & DESCRIPTIONS & PRICES

Sign Riders & Flyer Boxes

Every agent needs a safe supply of sign riders. Relatively inexpensive and generally sold at local associations, sign riders are a worthwhile investments. Sign riders are the small, usually hard or thin plastic or vinyl signs that hang from the bottom of the "For Sale" sign, hence, the term *sign riders*. Sign riders give the REALTOR® a chance to call extra attention to a specific feature of the property. For example, if the house has a swimming pool, you simply hang a sign rider that says "Swimming Pool." There are sign riders for virtually every feature or statement you can think of: spa, horse property, acreage, den, by appointment only, and more. One of the newer sign rider statements being made relate to technology. It is not at all unusual to see a "For Sale" sign that has an Internet address listed on the sign rider. While sign riders are really big business, and for good cause, they are limited to offering only small statements or features. One way to gain extra attention of passers by is to provide a flyer box on your For Sale sign.

Sign riders vary in price according to quality and size. Generally speaking, small sign riders are a couple of dollars, with the larger, more sturdy versions costing a few dollars more. Often times, if you are buying large quantities, discounts might apply.

Flyer boxes have become a near necessity. As we enter the technology era, note how buyers and sellers are well equipped with knowledge at the click of their mouse. This instant response mind-set has resulted in everything being immediate, and that's exactly where flyer boxes come into play. If someone is passing by your listing and thinks the house looks fairly nice, but the person is not quite motivated enough to pick up the phone....or, someone drives by the property and doesn't want to wait to place a call, but rather wants an immediate response, a flyer box is great. Flyer boxes might be sturdy, weatherproof acrylic, or may instead by flyer "pouches," which are thin flexible pouches that attach to the For Sale sign.

Obviously the more sturdy flyer boxes are more expensive, generally about $12-15, and the pouch shouldn't run you more than $5-7.

Flyer boxes are excellent marketing tools because you can provide potential buyers with just about any information you'd like, and of course, you'll include your own contact information so that when they decide to look at the inside of the property, you'll be the one that they call.

Calculators & Measuring Devices

While a standard calculator might suffice for balancing your checkbook, why not streamline your mortgage and interest related calculations with one that is specifically designed to do just that? There are many real estate calculators available and prices range roughly from $35-$50. A high-quality calculator should last you a substantial period of time. There are a few high-quality calculators are that worthy of mention here: Texas Instruments, Real Estate Master IIx and Qualifer Plus IIx.

The day of the difficult-to-bend metal tape measure is over. Now available and adored by REALTORS® around the country are electronic measuring devices. These devices no longer require you to get down on your hands and knees or even ask your clients for assistance when measuring rooms. You literally point at the wall you want measured and watch the magic. There are various types and features, so make sure you invest in one that accomplishes what you need. The price range for a high quality measuring device should be in the $40-60 price range.

REALTOR® Wear

Because agents are constantly marketing themselves to the public, one of the best avenues is to simply *wear* your work! Selective and high quality apparel that includes, polo shirts, jackets, sweatshirts, tee-shirts, baseball jerseys, baseball caps, brief cases, tote bags, and business professional and casual wear is now available to you. Not only are REALTORS® nationwide taking great advantage of this advertising opportunity, but they are recognizing the importance of organized real estate and thereby promoting it by proudly wearing the registered trademark that is only allowed to members of local, state, and national associations.

In addition, you can purchase jewelry, tie-tacks, and, watches that also feature the REALTOR® logo (which is trademarked by the NATIONAL ASSOCIATION OF REALTORS ®). For a great and exclusive selection of these products, visit the two websites that are referred to in the Web Resource section, Appendix B.

Appointment Book & Stationery

You will always want to have stationery and stamps on hand. Whether you are congratulating someone for something you just noted in the paper, or thanking a buyer for letting you show them property, you will be sending out too many notes to buy them one at a time. You can visit your local stationery store or look for online resources. Remember that what you send your clients and prospective clients says a lot about who you are. Write neatly and use high-quality supplies.

Appointment books come in too many sizes and varieties to note here. There are good reliable companies that are strictly committed to keeping you on schedule. They have put research time and dollars into providing you with a planning system they hope will keep you productive. As with many things, this is a personal choice. Some REALTORS® find the simplicity of a one-month per page adequate, while others rely on an intricate detail day-by-day description. Also, size should be considered. If you carry your calendar with you, as most agents do, you'll want something that isn't terribly heavy and won't fall apart if it hits the floor (and it will when you drop it!).

Good appointment books are worth their weight in gold and you might spend over $50 to find one that works well for you. It may seem expensive, but this is merely one of your annual expenses that will pay off in the long run.

SOFTWARE

Technology is always changing and new software products are hitting the shelves each day. It would therefore be impossible to cover all the software programs available that might help to streamline your business. Instead, we'll stick to those few that have stood the test of time, and were continually referenced by agents nationwide.

TOP PRODUCER™-Available nationwide, this is a CMA program that is capable of performing more real estate related assistance than most people can fathom. An agent could literally manage his or her entire business by using this program. The basics include: contact management, flyers, appointments, follow up assistance, and calculations. This is just the beginning though of what this number one real estate software can do to make your life as a REALTOR® more productive.

ZIPFORMS® or WINForms® 2000-Available nationwide (outside of California look for ZIPFORMS®, within California, WINForms®2000) this is the leader of the electronic forms movement. Clearly, e-commerce will play a critical role in the coming years of the real estate industry. If you begin now to take advantage of the time and cost effective methods available by using electronic forms, you will better prepared for the future. Furthermore, there is absolutely no comparison to a contract that has been scrawled out by hand, to the professional appeal of a printed form. Using this product will undoubtedly impress clients, other agents, and everyone involved in the real estate transaction.

MAPPING SOFTWARE-Available in various forms and for different states. Generally speaking, mapping software is in addition to or in lieu of the traditional map book that REALTORS® far and wide have come to rely on, and usually keep in their car. The convenience comes from being able to type in the destination and be given explicit directions to the property you are seeking. This isn't a software that's necessary for real estate sales, however, for a time effective means of planning your route, it's a worthwhile investment. (for this purpose, also consider a few of the very helpful mapping websites that offer this same service for free).

Again, visiting local, state, and national events, trade shows, tech fairs, and even your stationary store, can keep you up to date as to the latest and greatest, tools, services, and products, all intended to streamline your business.

APPENDIX B

WEBSITE REFERENCE GUIDE

There are literally hundreds of websites that contain a reference to real estate. Just type "real estate" in your Internet browser search field and prepare to be overwhelmed. Because there are so many sites, and because you are too busy listing properties and showing homes to explore them all, here is a list of relevant websites that will serve you well. As noted earlier, websites pop up all over the place every day, however, there are some sites that are more valuable than others. Make sure the sites you are visiting and spending your precious time "surfing" contain information that is of specific value to you. In addition to the URL's listed below, note the blank lines so that you may add your own, later on, as they might surface. Keep this book close to your computer as a constant source of referral.

Bookmark Your Favorites

When you find a website you like, you should only have to type the address in one time. This is the beauty of the "Favorite" feature on your Internet browser home page. Simply click the "Favorites" button and then click "Add to favorites" and the site that you are on will be automatically added to your "Favorites" folder. You can even change and add new folders that reflect something you will recognize more easily, such as "Real Estate Products," "Real Estate News," or something else that represents the content of the site that you find useful. Then, whenever you are online and would like to visit one of your favorite real estate sites, you'll simply look inside the "Favorites" folder of your choice and click on your selection.

WEBSITES TO KNOW

www.OneREALTORPlace.com

This is the NATIONAL ASSOCIATION of REALTORS® official website. Here you will find many resources for your professionally related needs and interests This includes, education, products (http://realtorteamstore.com/ for apparel), publications, service providers, real estate related news updates, convention and event updates, and access to the state associations all around the country. There are additional great finds on this site and it should be one you visit frequently to help keep yourself up to speed on the fast-pace of the real estate industry.

http://www.teamstoreonline.com/

Here is the place to purchase real estate related products, tools, and publications. This is also the place where you can locate REALTOR® gifts and apparel. This nationwide website is the absolute *must* for real estate professionals. Here you can find logo-apparel and products that help promote you as a real estate professional. Besides the fun and promotional items, the more traditional products like calculators, measuring devices, sign riders, and other tools, are available for purchase. Furthermore, this is the resource for corporate branding, great contests, special discounts for REALTOR® members, and a vast array of products.

www.inmannews.com

Inman news is a real estate news website that produces new industry-related articles daily. An excellent site to learn about what's going on in the industry and how it might affect you and the way you do business. There are literally hundreds of articles each days that concern local, state, and federal real estate issues and interests.

www.homestore.com

This website is created for the home buying and selling public, but it is a great site for agents to be familiar with, as it provides opportunities to promote listings world-wide.

www.winforms.com

This is the site for electronic forms within the state of California. The same product in all other states can be found at:

www.zipforms.com

www.frogpondgroup.com

This is a fun and informative site that serves as a great resource for agents, brokers, associations, and other industry professionals. Not only does it contain a wealth of real estate related news, but you can also find wonderful information on motivational speakers and other topics that virtually all real estate professionals possess an interest in.

Additional Websites (you want to remember):

_____

_____

_____

_____
_____
_____
_____
_____
_____
_____
_____
_____

Appendix C

RECOMMENDED READING

There is a host of reading material easily available for any agent wishing to learn more about the real estate industry, or to simply become and remain more motivated in selling efforts, and communication skills. This list is by no means exhaustive! Visit some of the websites noted earlier for even more titles that are coming out each year.

Real Estate Related Books, by Title only (look on teamstoreonline.com)
How Real Estate Agents Earn Big
Targeting the Over-55 Client,
English Spanish Real estate Glossary
Real Estate Marketing
Internet Marketing in Real Estate
Fight Foreclosure
The Commercial Guide Lease Book
Street Talk in Real Estate
The New Home Buying Strategy
Inside a Probate Sale, and Real Estate Agent's Guide
Wealth By Land
The Equity Sharing Book
Families on the Move
The Realty Blue Book
The Department of Real Estate Law Book (published every few years and sometimes available on disk)

Self-Protection for the Real Estate Professional
The Real Estate Book,
Bell's Guide: The Comprehensive Real Estate Handbook
Successful Farming By Mail
Successful Farming By phone
2,001 Winning Ads in Real Estate
Feng Shui, by Sheldon Hodge
Creative Real Estate Advertising Made Easy
From Ads to Riches
Power Real Estate Letters-includes disk with template letters

Finance Related Books (check www.amazon.com or your local bookstore)
The 9 Steps to Financial Freedom, by Suze Orman
Real Estate Professional's Tax Record

Motivational Books
Getting To Yes
Seat of the Soul
Meeting People and Influencing Friends
Think and Grow Rich
The Biology of Success
How to Sell Anything to Anyone

Communication Books
Lions Don't Need to Roar
Dealing with People You Can't Stand
Communicating at Work